RICHARD THE LIONHEART

Covering one of the most fascinating yet misunderstood periods in history, the MEDIEVAL LIVES series presents medieval people, concepts and events, drawing on political and social history, philosophy, material culture (art, architecture and archaeology) and the history of science. These books are global and wide-ranging in scope, encompassing both Western and non-Western subjects, and span the fifth to the fifteenth centuries, tracing significant developments from the collapse of the Roman Empire onwards.

SERIES EDITOR: Deirdre Jackson

RICHARD THE LIONHEART

In Life and in Legend

HEATHER BLURTON

REAKTION BOOKS

To my Dad, Keith Blurton

Published by Reaktion Books Ltd
2–4 Sebastian Street
London EC1V OHE, UK
www.reaktionbooks.co.uk

First published 2025
Copyright © Heather Blurton 2025

EU GPSR Authorised Representative
Logos Europe, 9 rue Nicolas Poussin, 17000, La Rochelle, France
email: contact@logoseurope.eu

Printed and bound in India by Replika Press Pvt. Ltd

A catalogue record for this book is available from the British Library

ISBN 978 1 83639 123 4

CONTENTS

Statue of Richard the Lionheart by Carlo Marochetti, 1856, outside the Houses of Parliament, London.

Introduction: The Life and Times of Richard I

How did a king who once boasted that he would sell London if he could find someone to buy it come to be lauded as the flower of English chivalry, one of the most famous English kings, and a figure of legend? This book explores the enigmatic figure of King Richard I of England (1157–1199): a crusader king who ruled over most of present-day England, Ireland and France. Richard famously spent less than six months of his reign in England and probably did not even speak English, but his statue now stands outside the Houses of Parliament in Westminster as a model of English kingship and national pride. Much like Alexander the Great and Charlemagne, he is a historical figure who has entered the annals of legend, although he is perhaps more akin to the mythical King Arthur for the way in which his legend has stood the test of time and, indeed, evolved with it.

Like King Arthur, Richard the Lionheart has a long afterlife across media – in literature, art and film. Richard's apotheosis even began in his own lifetime, stage-managed at least in part by the king himself. His exploits were praised and critiqued by chroniclers who accompanied him on crusade and by the troubadours who enlivened the courts of southern France. Centuries after his death he lived on as the hero of romance and as the champion of Robin Hood and his Merry Men. In the nineteenth century Sir Walter Scott returned to the figure of Richard the

Lionheart with his seminal novels *Ivanhoe* (1819) and *The Talisman* (1825). Richard the Lionheart features alongside Robin Hood in some of the very earliest motion pictures, as well as in contemporary blockbusters. Most recently, he has been immortalized in the video game *Assassin's Creed*. Richard's long life as a literary figure far exceeds the length and import of his ten-year reign. It is particularly interesting that literary representations of Richard often appear at moments of literary innovation, at the birth of new genres: in the earliest vernacular poetry in French, for example, in the earliest novels, in the earliest motion pictures. There is something about the figure of Richard the Lionheart that lends itself to innovation alongside continuity. This book, therefore, is a history not only of the life and times of Richard I, but of the stories that were told about him, beginning in his own lifetime and traced through the centuries that followed.

Many of the stories that have been told about Richard over the course of centuries have very little connection to the realities of Richard's own life, or to the world in which he lived. Therefore, before we turn to the literature that immortalized him, it is necessary to lay out the contours of the history of his biography. This introduction will describe what we know about the life and times of Richard I, noting where historians – both medieval and modern – disagree about the historical record. By any account, his life and times were remarkable.

Richard I of England was born in 1157 into an extraordinary family: 'His ancestors on both sides', notes the French historian Jean Flori with some understatement, 'were endowed with strong personalities.'[1] His father, Henry II, inherited his claim to the throne of England through his mother, the empress Matilda. Matilda was the daughter of Henry I of England, and she styled herself 'Empress' throughout her life, owing to her first marriage to Holy Roman Emperor Henry V. Henry II was her son from her second marriage, to Geoffrey of Anjou. Although Henry 1 had named Matilda as his heir, and demanded that his barons swear fealty to her, after his death she was unable to secure the throne from its rival claimant, King Stephen, whose claim also descended through his mother, Adele of Blois, a sister of Henry 1. However, Matilda – and subsequently her son Henry – never ceased to assert her claim over the throne that was rightfully hers. The period of their conflict is termed 'the Anarchy', and is described poignantly by one contemporary chronicler as a time 'when men said openly that Christ and his saints slept'.[2] When, in 1153, Stephen's only son, Eustace, died, he and Henry 11 came to an agreement that Stephen would rule during his lifetime, naming Henry as his heir. As fate or luck would have it, Stephen passed away shortly thereafter. In 1154 Henry was crowned king of England and thus came to rule over what historians have termed the Angevin Empire, encompassing England, Ireland, Wales, Normandy, Anjou and the lands of Aquitaine, where his wife, Eleanor, had become duchess in 1137 – which is to say, all of England and most of France.

In 1152 Henry had married Eleanor of Aquitaine, heiress to vast territories in the South of France. She, too, was from an illustrious lineage. Eleanor's grandfather William 1x, duke of Aquitaine, is famous as the 'first troubadour'. Moreover, her first husband was King Louis v11 of France. Historians have long suggested that his monkish character was at odds with Eleanor's more worldly temperament, and that this mismatch contributed to the failure of the marriage. At first, however, the signs were auspicious. Eleanor even accompanied her husband on the Second Crusade. The chronicler William of Newburgh describes, perhaps optimistically, how

> initially she had so enmeshed and captivated the heart of
> the young man with the charm of her beauty that when he

The Angevin Empire.

was about to embark on that most celebrated expedition
his over-urgent longing for his young wife led him to
decide that she should certainly not be left at home,
but should set out with him to the wars.[3]

The marriage broke down shortly afterwards. Although the
couple were reconciled by the pope long enough to have a second
daughter, the marriage was annulled. The official reason was
consanguinity, since Eleanor and Louis were cousins in the fourth
and fifth degree, and, although rumours of infidelity subsequently
circulated, modern historians have suggested that the real problem may have been the failure of the marriage to provide a male
heir to the throne of France. The fifteen-year marriage produced
two daughters: Marie de Champagne and Alix de Blois.

Whatever the case, the ink was scarcely dry on the annulment
decree before Eleanor married Henry, then duke of Normandy,
but shortly to become king of England. With Henry being somewhat closer to Eleanor in temperament, this marriage was either
passionate or tumultuous, depending on one's point of view. It
produced eight children: five sons and three daughters. But it
also produced strife. Estranged from Henry, Eleanor supported
her sons in their failed rebellion against their father, and, for
her trouble, ended up imprisoned for the last sixteen years of
their marriage. When Henry died in 1189, the first act of his heir,
Richard, was to release his mother from captivity.

Rumours, especially allegations of infidelity, swirled around
Eleanor, as they often do with powerful women. The most famous of the rumours, which circulated within her lifetime, was that
she had an affair with her own uncle, Raymond of Antioch, while
on crusade with Louis. The twelfth-century chronicler Richard
of Devizes notes coyly: 'Many know what I wish none of us knew.
The same queen, during the time of her first husband, was at
Jerusalem. Let no one say any more about it. I know it well. Keep

silent!'[4] Of course, no one did keep silent, and stories about the divorce became more and more salacious over the course of the twelfth century. By the thirteenth century, after Eleanor's death, legend had it that she had had an affair with Saladin, the sultan of Egypt and Syria.[5] Nearly two hundred years after her death she remains the subject of yet another set of scandalous rumours: that she had her husband's mistress, 'the Fair Rosamund', cruelly murdered. This rumour first appears nearly two hundred years after Eleanor's death, in the *French Chronicle of London*. Building on the monk Ranulf Higden's fourteenth-century story that Henry hid Rosamund in a secret bower, over the course of the early modern period the legend was elaborated until the beautiful Rosamund became the true love of Henry's life, and he hid her away in a labyrinth; the jealous Eleanor, Theseus-like, solved the mystery of the labyrinth by following a silken thread and poisoned the fair Rosamund. These rumours tell us more about the discomfort of medieval clerical culture with women's access to political and economic power than they do about Eleanor. But the point is that Richard was born into a family that seemed made for legend, and around which fantastic stories tended to accumulate.

Richard was not expected to become king. At the time of his birth a first-born son, William, had died in early childhood, but another son, Henry, survived and was heir to his father's throne. He had six surviving siblings, all of whom had illustrious careers of their own. These were younger brothers Geoffrey, count of Brittany, and John, ultimately Richard's successor as king; and sisters Matilda (future wife of Henry the Lion, duke of Saxony), Eleanor (future wife of King Alfonso VIII of Castile and grandmother of St Louis IX of France), and Joan (future wife of King William of Sicily and subsequently Count Raymond VI of Toulouse). Henry II ruled over a large and diverse territory, and by 1168 he had four surviving sons. He began to plan a slow devolution of power to them. Or perhaps not really a devolution, since Henry intended to keep the power. But he, in a sense, earmarked the portions of his territory that he intended for his sons. For his heir, his eldest son, Henry, the patrimony: Anjou and Maine, Normandy and England. For Richard, the second son, his mother's patrimony of Aquitaine. The third son, Geoffrey, had married the heiress to Brittany, so would inherit that through his wife. For John, the youngest, the county of Mortain in northwestern France (later, after Henry's conquest of Ireland, that territory would also be earmarked for John). Thus when Henry II fell ill in 1170 he decided to put this planned devolution of power into action. Richard's brother Henry was crowned king alongside his father, in an imitation of the French tradition of crowning the heir to the throne while his predecessor was still reigning. Henceforth he would be known as 'the Young King' to distinguish him from his father. While his brother was crowned king, Richard went to Aquitaine with Eleanor to take up his new position. There he held a Christmas court in 1171 and the following summer was invested as duke of Aquitaine and count of Poitou at the Abbey of Sainte-Hilaire in Poitiers. He was fifteen years old.

Their father, meanwhile, recovered his health and with it his appetite for power. This caused significant friction between him and his sons. Newly crowned, the Young King chafed at bearing his title in name only, with none of the attendant power. Richard had something of the opposite problem; while his mother fully intended that he should be duke in fact as well as in name, his father did not appreciate the large, wealthy and strategically important duchy of Aquitaine being alienated from his control. Then there was the problem of his brother John, upon whom Henry II proposed to settle some castles that the Young King felt were part of his own inheritance. Finally, Geoffrey was still having to wait to marry Constance, the heiress of Brittany, so he could begin ruling her lands. All this and more came to a head in 1173, when Henry II's three oldest sons allied with his wife in rebellion against him. Henry, Richard and Geoffrey went to their father's old enemy, Louis VII of France, for shelter and support, and they received it. Although initially successful, by 1174 the rebellion had failed. Richard – who at first attempted to keep the rebellion alive in Aquitaine – realized the game was up once Louis made peace with Henry II, and he threw himself at his father's feet and begged for forgiveness. Richard and his brothers were reconciled with their father, and Eleanor was effectively placed under house arrest in England for the remainder of Henry II's life.

In the wake of the rebellion, Richard seems to have returned his full support to his father. One cost of this reconciliation was Richard being charged with re-establishing order in his domains in Aquitaine. In the second half of the 1170s and the early 1180s, Richard had great success recruiting a mercenary army, besieging and reducing castles, taking captives and generally turning against

Church of Saint-Hilaire le Grand, Poitiers.

his former allies, those barons who had previously supported him in his rebellion against his father. It was during these campaigns that Richard established himself as a warrior and strategist on a par with his father, and it was during these campaigns that the nickname 'Lionheart' took hold. The historian Gerald of Wales called him 'our lion' and later, while on crusade, the chronicler Ambroise called him 'lionheart'.[6] In these years he consolidated his reputation as a fearsome warrior and a somewhat brutal and despotic ruler. Historians have noted that it was during these years that cracks began to appear in the relationship between Richard and Henry, the Young King. Henry was, on several occasions, sent to Richard's aid, and on those occasions had the opportunity to become envious not only of Richard's splendid lifestyle as count of Poitou but, perhaps more importantly, of his greater autonomy from their father. There was a squabble about whether or not Richard should have to pay homage to his elder brother. In 1182, when yet another rebellion broke out in Aquitaine, Henry and Richard's brother Geoffrey joined the cause of the counts of Limoges and Angoulême against Richard. While Richard appealed to his father for help against his brothers, the Young King Henry appealed for help to Philip Augustus, now king of France after the death of his father. Just when history seemed bound to repeat itself by pitting the king of England against the king of France, the Young King Henry died, at only 27 years of age. The troubadour Bertran de Born, who was himself involved in the conflict, penned a touching tribute to Henry:

> For evermore I close my song in grief and think it ended,
> for I have lost my subject and my joy and the best king
> ever of a mother born – generous and well spoken, and
> a good horseman, handsome, and humble in conferring
> great honours. I fear that grief torments me so much that
> it will choke me, for I talk about it unceasingly.[7]

The Young King's death left Richard as Henry II's oldest
surviving son, but, since he was already installed as duke of
Aquitaine, his ascension to the throne of England was not fully
assured. Henry II initially suggested that Richard take up the
Young King's previous role and territories, as a sort of king-in-
waiting, but that in doing so he surrender Aquitaine to his youngest brother, John. Richard refused, angrily, and another round of
family strife and warfare ensued, a jockeying for position and
territory. This time the crisis was resolved by Richard paying homage to his mother – temporarily released from her political exile
– for Aquitaine, thus acknowledging her as its true lord, but really
acknowledging that the power lay in his father's hands. Geoffrey
remained in revolt against Richard and his father; he wanted to
extend his territory from Brittany into at least part of the neigh-
bouring Anjou, and he was supported by Philip Augustus, who
made him seneschal, a kind of chief administrator, of France. It
was during this unrest, however, that Geoffrey also died, thrown
from his horse during a tournament (or more prosaically, according to one chronicler, of illness). One contemporary describes
Philip as so distressed by this death that he had to be restrained
from throwing himself into Geoffrey's grave. In the space of three
years Henry II had lost two sons. Gerald of Wales writes that 'the
father's grief could not be compared to any other; for there was
no grief like his grief.'[8]

Following Geoffrey's death, the tension between Henry II and
Philip of France threatened once again to erupt into war, but
Richard assumed the role of mediator and brokered a truce
between the two kings. He subsequently returned with Philip to
Paris, where the two men were seen to be on increasingly intimate
terms. The diplomat and chronicler Roger of Howden writes that

Richard, earl of Poitou, remained with the king of France,
though much against the will of his father, and the king of

France held him in such high esteem, that every day they ate at the same table and from the same dish, and at night had not separate chambers. In consequence of this strong attachment which seemed to have risen between them, the king of England was struck with great astonishment, and wondered what it could mean.[9]

This report of the closeness at this time between Richard and Philip, alongside other similar mentions by twelfth-century writers – including an anecdote in which a pious hermit threatens Richard with the story of Sodom and Gomorrah – has led to the suggestion by some modern historians that Richard may have enjoyed sexual relations with men. Indeed, the translation 'strong attachment' above does not quite express the strength of the original Latin words *vehementem amorem*, which are perhaps better translated as 'vehement love'.[10] First published in 1948, the claim has been debated ever since, and it has strongly influenced the representation of Richard in modern film and literature, as in *The Lion in Winter* (dir. Anthony Harvey, 1968) and Jean

Saladin capturing the Holy Cross from Guy of Lusignan at the Battle of Hattin in 1187, marginalia from Matthew Paris, *Chronica maiora*, 13th century.

Plaidy's historical romance *The Heart of the Lion* (1977), for example. If we listen to the twelfth-century chronicles, we are left with the impression that whatever the truth may have been concerning Richard's sexuality, it did not significantly affect their assessment of him as a king and crusader, or, indeed, as a man.[11]

In any case, this relative quiet was soon shattered by news from Jerusalem. On 4 July 1187 disaster struck. The Battle of Hattin, a pitched battle between the forces of Guy of Lusignan (king of Jerusalem) and Saladin (sultan of Egypt and Syria), ended in the utter defeat of the crusader army and the fall of Jerusalem shortly thereafter. The Kingdom of Jerusalem had been established in 1099 as a result of the First Crusade. The Crusades – military expeditions, imagined as armed pilgrimages, to the Holy Land, starting at the end of the eleventh century – had hoped, in the first instance, to 'liberate' Jerusalem from Muslim control. In this regard, the First Crusade had been wildly successful. In addition to the Kingdom of Jerusalem, three other Crusader 'states' were established, set up under the control of Western leaders: the Principality of Antioch, the County of Edessa and the County of Tripoli. However, these new territories were held only with difficulty. Edessa fell in 1146, catalysing the disastrous Second Crusade (on which Richard's mother, Eleanor, had accompanied her first husband), which failed to reconquer the territory. When Jerusalem subsequently fell in 1187, the shock reverberated throughout Europe.

Richard immediately took the cross and pledged to go on crusade to recapture Jerusalem. Before he could make good on his vow, however, his situation changed dramatically. Tension flared again between Richard and his barons, between Richard and his father, and between Richard, Philip and Henry. Exasperated at his father's refusal to acknowledge him formally as his heir, Richard paid homage to the French king. Gerald of Wales described the situation:

the count of Poitou [that is, Richard] went over to the
king of France then and there before his father's eyes,
since he had not been able to obtain from his father by
his entreaties either previously or now the fealty of the
chief men, and so was suspicious of him and his malice,
since he was always resentful of his successor and was
attempting to put the younger born ahead of the heirs,
to their loss, and he immediately performed homage
to the king of France for the Continental lands that
pertained to him by hereditary right. Moreover, after
they had bound themselves together in an alliance with
the mutual bonds of oaths, the king entered into a solemn
promise to help the count to get hold of those Continental
lands from his father, and, because of this, inexorable
discord arose at that time, and such implacable strife
was set in motion that it did not end until the father
came to his last day.[12]

Finally, after two years of warfare, on 4 July 1189 Henry II was
defeated by the joint forces of his eldest son and his oldest enemy.
Roger of Howden describes a dramatic scene as Philip and Henry
met to make peace, accompanied by such frightening portents
as thunder emanating from a clear sky and a thunderbolt striking
the ground between the two kings. As the terms of peace were
concluded, Henry asked for a list of all the men who had betrayed
him and sided with Philip and Richard. He was broken-hearted
to find at the top of the list the name of his youngest and favourite son, John.[13] He died days later. Several chroniclers describe
the scene of Richard visiting his father's body as it lay at rest at
the abbey of Fontevraud; as Richard approached, blood flowed
out of Henry's nostrils, expressing the age-old tradition that
corpses will bleed in the presence of their murderers, an implicit
accusation against Richard. Nevertheless, when Richard finally

set out on crusade in the autumn of 1190, he went as king of England.

But first, Richard had to consolidate his power over his new realm. His first act as king was to release his mother from the imprisonment she had suffered since the rebellion against the old king. And among her first acts was to release all prisoners in the kingdom, since, as the later chronicler Matthew Paris commented, she knew well the pain of captivity.[14] Sixty-seven years old at the time, she seems to have picked up where she left off, acting, to all intents and purposes, as if she were still queen of England. Richard was invested as duke of Normandy on 20 July 1189, and crowned king of England in September that year. He was well received in England, and his lavish coronation ceremony is described by Roger of Howden. After a long procession, led by the clergy and the highest nobility, Richard arrived at the altar of Westminster Abbey:

> kneeling before the altar, with the holy Evangelists placed before him, and many relics of the saints, according to custom, he swore that he would all the days of his life observe peace, honour, and reverence towards God, the Holy Church, and its ordinances. He also swore that he would exercise true justice and equity towards the people committed to his charge. He also swore that he would abrogate bad laws and unjust customs, if any such had been introduced into his kingdom, and would enact good laws, and observe the same without fraud or evil intent.[15]

After these oaths were taken, he was anointed with holy oil and clothed in royal robes. He was given golden spurs, the sword of rule and, finally, the crown, rod and sceptre. Roger reported that the crown was so heavy that its weight had to be supported by two earls. After the ceremony, the coronation was celebrated with a feast.

As several chroniclers describe, if Richard's coronation was accompanied by celebrations, it was also attended by bloodshed. Richard had evidently excluded both women and Jews from his coronation feast. Scholars debate whether the exclusion of women from English coronations was traditional, but it does not seem that the exclusion of Jews was. Whatever the case, when some of London's leading Jewish citizens attempted to offer the new king gifts, they were attacked by those present. The situation soon spiralled out of control as Londoners attacked the Jewish quarter of the city and set it on fire. Some accounts say that the new king personally attempted to intervene to stop the violence. According to Roger,

> On the day after the coronation, the king sent his servants, and caused those offenders to be arrested who had set fire to the city; not for the sake of the Jews, but on account of the houses and property of the Christians which they had burnt and plundered, and he ordered some of them to be hanged.[16]

Despite Richard's issuing a royal writ of protection for the Jews, the violence was not contained in London, and subsequently pogroms against the Jews were set off across the country. These culminated in a terrible scene in York, where Jews attempted to seek refuge in the royal castle. Besieged, and finding their situation hopeless, they committed mass suicide. Those who attempted to leave the castle were murdered as they did so. These events give some sense of the mood in England, and in Europe, on the eve of another crusade. There were those who felt that Europe's 'enemies within' should be defeated before the enemy without was confronted. Violence against European Jews was a

common aspect of crusading culture, and crusades were subsequently unleashed within Europe at 'heretical' Christian populations, such as the Albigensians, or Cathars, of southern
France.[17]

As soon after his coronation as he was able, Richard left on
crusade. Crusading was an expensive endeavour, and Henry II
had tried to prepare for the expense by means of levying a 10 per
cent tax on revenue and movable property. The tax soon came
to be known as 'the Saladin tithe', and it met with predictable
complaints. Matthew Paris clearly expressed the general feeling
on the subject when he described it as 'robbery'.[18] But Richard
needed even more than this to finance his crusade, funds he
raised by selling land and offices back to their original holders.
It was during this fundraising drive that he cracked his famous
joke about being willing to sell London if he could only find a
buyer.

If Richard's finances needed to be sorted out, so too did his
succession. Who would rule while he was on crusade, and, perhaps most importantly, who would rule if he failed to return? His
younger brother Geoffrey had left a male heir, Arthur of Brittany,
but Arthur was still a child. Richard's youngest brother, John,
was waiting in the wings, but Richard did not trust him. Richard
had recently renewed his promise to Philip that he would marry
Philip's sister Alice, to whom he had been betrothed since childhood, but he was reluctant to do so (perhaps owing to rumours
that she had been his father's mistress). In the event, he left
Eleanor as a sort of regent, supported by an aristocrat, Hugh de
Puiset, and an ecclesiast, William Longchamp, Bishop of Ely.

Richard was not alone in embarking on crusade. He joined
Philip Augustus of France and the Holy Roman Emperor Fred-
erick Barbarossa (the latter of whom died en route). Although,
to be sure, Richard and Philip had a love/hate relationship, by
the time they were preparing to go on crusade, relations between

them had once again disintegrated. During his father's lifetime, Richard had often allied himself with Philip in order to strengthen his position against Henry. Now that he was king, however, he began to see the political situation more from his father's point of view, as he now held claim to the territories his father had contested with Philip. On the eve of their crusade, both men were so mistrustful of the other's ambitions that neither would go while the other stayed behind. So Richard and Philip set out together and agreed to rendezvous in Sicily before heading east. Through various delays and intrigues, their stay was longer than intended. During their sojourn in Sicily it began to become clear how difficult it would be to hold together the different Christian factions against their common enemy. English chroniclers describe Philip as continually attempting to undermine Richard. Violence broke out between the crusaders and the local populations, leading to bloodshed even before the crusaders had reached their destination.

While in Sicily Richard intended to collect his recently widowed sister, Joan (who had been married to the king of Sicily, William the Good), along with her dowry. It was in Sicily that the long engagement between Richard and Alice was finally ended, and Richard's mother personally delivered to him instead a different bride, Berengaria of Navarre. It was also in Sicily that one of the stranger episodes in the build-up to the crusade occurred: Richard's penance and meeting with the famous monk and theologian Joachim of Fiore. Richard was evidently stricken with remorse for some unnamed sin (generally interpreted to be of a lustful nature) and, hoping to approach either the imminent Christmas season or his crusade – or both – with pure conscience and soul, he performed a public penance. 'From that hour', says Roger of Howden, he 'became a man who feared God, and left what was evil and did what was good'.[19] It was just after this episode that Richard reached out to Joachim, with whom he had a long conversation about Joachim's interpretation of the Book of Revelation. Such a preoccupation with the end times is perhaps appropriate in a man embarking on crusade, and, indeed, Joachim had identified Saladin as the Antichrist in one of his prophecies.

A second detour on Richard's journey east had similarly unanticipated consequences: the conquest of Cyprus and its establishment as a Latin – which is to say, western European – kingdom. A storm at sea blew the ships off course, and the ship carrying Richard's sister and fiancée was wrecked on the island of Cyprus and its contents plundered by the locals. Richard complained to the island's ruler, Isaac Comnenus, a member of the Byzantine imperial family who proved to be unhelpful. Angered, Richard turned his crusading army against Isaac, and conquered the island in less than a week. When Isaac begged not to be clapped in iron shackles, Richard reportedly had him put in chains of silver. This victory seemed an auspicious start to Richard's crusade, and it burnished his coffers as well as his reputation.

Although the Third Crusade was not the great success Richard no doubt hoped for, neither was it a total disaster. Richard arrived at the siege of Acre somewhat glamorously, having sunk one of Saladin's supply ships on the way into the harbour. Acre was a strategically and economically important port city, and it was the main avenue through which crusaders could receive supplies from the West. At the time of Richard's arrival crusading forces had been besieging the city for a year. It surrendered to the crusaders only one month after Richard's arrival. During the siege, however, both Philip Augustus and Richard became sick. After the situation was resolved, Philip decided that he wanted to return to France: probably because of the repeated recurrence of his illness, but also because the death of Count Philip of Flanders from sickness at Acre altered the balance of power on the home front. Richard reluctantly agreed to release him from their crusading pact, but in return asked him to agree to a pact of non-aggression towards Richard's lands on the Continent for the duration of Richard's crusade. Richard remained suspicious of Philip, not least because back home his brother John kept trying to seize control of the government of England.

With Philip's departure, Richard was the undisputed leader of the crusading armies. Although the retreat of the French king had the advantage of reserving all the power and glory for Richard, his first major act was not at all glorious. As both sides hesitated in fulfilling the agreed terms upon the surrender of Acre to the crusading armies, and amid a climate of mistrust between Richard

Acre surrendering to Philip and Richard, miniature from *Grandes chroniques de France*, 1375–80.

and Saladin, Richard ordered the execution of his Muslim hostages, more than 2,000 of them. This horrific act troubled even many contemporary chroniclers, both Muslim and Christian. Richard's reasoning for giving this order is still unclear. One Muslim chronicler opined:

> Many reasons were given to explain the massacre.
> One was that they had killed them in reprisal for
> their own prisoners whom Muslims had previously
> killed. Another was that the king of England had
> decided to march to Ascalon and did not want to
> leave so many prisoners behind in Acre. God alone
> knows what his reason really was![20]

The Christian chronicler Ambroise was clearer in his own estimation:

> But [in order to] bring down the pride of the Turks,
> disgrace their religion and avenge Christianity, he
> brought out of the town, in bonds, two thousand
> and seven hundred people who were all slaughtered.
> Thus was vengeance taken for the blows and the
> crossbow bolts. Thanks be to God the Creator.[21]

In response, Saladin executed his Christian hostages.

From Acre Richard headed to the coastal cities of Ascalon and Jaffa in order to secure the Mediterranean coast before attempting the inland – and extremely well-guarded – city of Jerusalem, which was the crusaders' ultimate goal. It was a difficult march, with Saladin's forces harrying the crusaders, who attempted to maintain discipline. Saladin bided his time while the crusading army slogged through the heat, then mounted an attack when they reached Arsuf. Richard and the crusaders won the battle decisively, and Richard himself also won renown as a disciplined and astute strategist.

Richard's strategic acumen, however, as much as it burnished his reputation in one regard, harmed it in another, because it prevented him from following popular – if reckless – opinion and attempting to take Jerusalem. Although he marched his army to within sight of the walls of that city, without the French forces who had left with Philip he lacked the manpower to protect his lengthy supply lines or to hold Jerusalem even if he had managed to capture it. At this point, divisions were starting to arise within the crusading armies: divisions between those who wanted to take Jerusalem at all costs, those who urged caution and those who identified other strategic locations – Egypt, for example – that would undermine Saladin's power. Despite his hesitation before Jerusalem, Richard achieved one of the most famous victories of his career when he attacked and decimated one of Saladin's supply caravans deep in the desert at al-Hasi. It is at this point that most historians – then and now – believe Richard had his best opportunity to succeed at capturing Jerusalem. But instead, he entered into negotiations with Saladin. The negotiations were extended and broke down more than once. At stake was more than territory. Almost as much as Jerusalem itself, the crusaders wanted the return of the True Cross – the relic of the cross on which Christ had been crucified – which had been captured along with Jerusalem by Saladin at the Battle of Hattin in 1187. Another sticking point included access to pilgrimage sites. At one point, Richard even proposed a marriage between his sister Joan and Saladin's brother (Joan, evidently, categorically refused to go along with the plan). Richard's problems were exacerbated by news that kept arriving from England: that his brother John, with the silent support of Philip, was conspiring to seize the throne, and that he was beginning to attract the support of the English barons. In the end, Richard concluded

a three-year truce with Saladin, and in 1192 he left the Holy
Land for ever.

What happened next is stranger than fiction. On his return
Richard was shipwrecked and forced to travel back to England
along the Adriatic coast, as Philip had fomented the barons of
Aquitaine into revolt against him, blocking his route through that
province. Indeed, from the moment of his return to France Philip
wasted no time in stirring up trouble for Richard. First he entered
into an alliance with the Holy Roman Emperor Henry VI. One
of Henry's vassals, Duke Leopold of Austria, had good reason
to despise Richard. As the leader of the German contingent at
the siege of Acre, Leopold felt he had earned a right to a share of
the victory and the spoils. Richard, however, disagreed, evidently
trampling Leopold's banner, along with his claims, underfoot,
and humiliating him. Moreover, there were rumours that Richard
had arranged for the murder of Conrad of Montferrat, newly
elected king of Jerusalem and Leopold's cousin, by the Islamic sect
the Assassins. Once ashore, Richard and his companions, therefore, found themselves in enemy territory. They were forced to
travel in disguise: some sources say as pilgrims, others as merchants. After narrowly escaping detection and arrest on several
occasions, Richard's luck ran out. There are various versions of
how his disguise was unmasked. In one a keen-eyed town guard
spotted the king's elaborately embroidered gloves tucked into his
servant's belt. The 'servant' was arrested and, under torture, con-
fessed all. In another version, Richard was discovered hiding in
a peasant's house, turning the spit as he prepared dinner for his
companions.[22] Once discovered, he arrogantly refused to surrender himself to anyone bar Duke Leopold himself. The duke quickly
obliged, and Richard became his prisoner. For more than a year
he was held hostage, first by Leopold, then by Henry VI.

Emperor Henry produced a litany of unfounded accusations
against Richard: that he had sold his army to Saladin; that he

Reliquary cross from the Guelph Treasure, first half of the 12th century.
Behind a square piece of rock crystal at the foot of the cross,
there is, purportedly, a fragment of the True Cross.

had had Conrad of Montferrat treacherously assassinated; that
he had even tried to have the king of France assassinated. In a
public trial that medieval chroniclers report dramatically, Richard
denied the accusations and made an eloquent speech in his own
defence. The emperor, as well as all those looking on, was impressed, and Richard subsequently remained on good terms with
Henry while his ransom was negotiated. The ransom was enormous: over 150,000 silver marks and more besides. It was collected
by a universal tax on Richard's kingdom, which even then was
not enough, so that churches were forced to liquidate the gold
and silver in their treasuries. But in February 1194 Richard was
finally back in England, where he made a triumphal entry into
London and staged a ceremonial crown-wearing at Winchester.
Upon his release, Philip wrote to John that 'the devil is loose.'
By May, Richard was back on the Continent. In his absence John
had been attempting to shore up support for his efforts to take
control of England by granting lands and castles to potential allies.
These included Philip of France, to whom John ceded most of
Normandy. Back in Normandy, however, Richard was reconciled
to John without incident. The short remainder of Richard's life
was spent reasserting his authority over his Continental possessions, warring with Philip Augustus and building Château
Gaillard, designed as the ultimate defence of Normandy.

As with so many aspects of his life, the story of Richard's
death has passed into legend. In 1199 Richard was besieging the
castle of Châlus-Chabrol, which was held by Aimar of Limoges.
Some chroniclers suggested that he was after a recently discovered treasure, but it is more likely that he wanted to regain control
of a strategically important castle. With the siege ongoing, one
evening Richard rode out to inspect the progress. An archer
defending the battlements – famously with only a saucepan for
a shield – saw his chance and took a pot shot at the king. Richard
was not wearing armour when the bolt struck him in the shoulder.

According to legend, amazed at this audacity, Richard congrat-
ulated the archer; he should not have. The bolt was difficult to extract and the wound turned gangrenous. Richard sent for his
mother, who arrived just in time to witness his death on 6 April
1199. With his death, Richard's contemporaries marked the
passing of a legend. When he wanted to give an example of the
literary device of sorrowful apostrophe, the rhetorician Geoffrey
of Vinsauf used the example of Richard's death: 'England, once
defended under the shield of Richard, now defenceless, witness
your sorrow with this lament: let tears ooze from your eyes; let
terror distend your lips; let twisting knot your fingers; let inner
sorrow bleed; and let wailing beat against the sky.'[23]

Later medieval kings were held up to Richard's example.[24] If
his contemporaries were certain of his greatness, however, historians have not always agreed with them. There has over the
centuries been significant disagreement among historians assess-
ing Richard's reign.[25] Some historians have felt that he neglected
England too much, that he simply used it as a piggy bank. When
the tide of opinion turned against crusading, the value of Richard's
reputation as a crusader faded. More recently, however, historians
have attempted to evaluate the relative success or failure of his
reign in terms of the expectations of his own culture. In his own
time, certainly, he was regarded as an epitome of chivalry. He was
believed to be generous, courageous and chivalric, if sometimes
choleric and brutal. As the historian John Gillingham describes,
even Muslim historians admired Richard. The thirteenth-century
writer Ibn al-Athir wrote: 'Richard's courage, shrewdness, energy
and patience made him the most remarkable ruler of his times.'[26]
He was also evidently quite handsome. One chronicler describes
him thus:

> He was tall, of elegant build; the colour of his hair was
> between red and gold; his limbs were supple and straight.

He had quite long arms, which were particularly
convenient for drawing a sword and wielding it most
effectively. His long legs matched the arrangement
of his whole body . . . His was a figure worthy to
govern.[27]

Modern-day studies of Richard I, such as John Gillingham's
Richard I and Jean Flori's *Richard the Lionheart: King and Knight*
(both 1999) – both of which offer eminently readable histories
of Richard's life and times – have focused on reassessing his reign,
which was, by any standards, remarkable. However, such studies
have been most interested in separating fact from fiction. The
chapters that follow will focus on the fiction. The biography of
Richard I described in this Introduction, for example, is garnered
largely from the words of medieval historians who were Richard's
contemporaries, some of whom knew him and had even been on
crusade with him. Nevertheless, the conventions and expectations associated with historical writing were different from
today's, and these medieval histories therefore pose problems of
interpretation for scholars who seek to use them to uncover the
facts of Richard's reign. The first chapter considers the medieval
histories that recount his reign from the point of view of their
genres – chronicle, epic, satire. As much as writers contemporary
to Richard the Lionheart describe his exploits, they are simultaneously using those exploits as a pattern and provocation to
literary expression. This chapter explores the ways in which
twelfth-century writers responded to the provocation that was
Richard I.

Alongside history writing, the second half of the twelfth
century brought a new literary tradition to western Europe: literature in the vernacular Romance languages and the (re)birth
of fiction in the secular literature of courtly love. These new
genres focused on secular experience and particularly on love

as an individual and social good. They found expression in French rather than in Latin, and they were designed for aristocratic audiences as leisure activities. This efflorescence of literary production has long been connected with the Angevin Empire, whose rulers Henry II and Eleanor of Aquitaine, Marie de Champagne (Eleanor's daughter by her first marriage) and Richard were all active patrons of history, poetry and romance. The earliest of these vernacular literary traditions was the troubadour poetry of the South of France. Richard is a frequent subject (and target) of troubadour verses. This book's second chapter reads the representation of Richard across the poetry of the troubadours Marcabrun, Bernart de Ventadorn, Peire Vidal, Bertran de Born, Guiraut de Borneil and Raimbaut de Vaqueiras, who wrote both for and about him. This gives insight into not only how Richard was perceived by his contemporaries but the development of the twin themes of troubadour poems: politics and love. The chapter concludes with two poems attributed to Richard himself: the prison lament 'Ja nus hons pris' and the political *sirventes* (service song) 'Dalfin je us voill desrenier'. More than a century after his death, Richard the Lionheart returns as the hero of romance in the Middle English *Richard Coeur de Lion*. The third chapter discusses this romance's use of the memory of Richard. Set during Richard's battles with Saladin for control of Jerusalem during the Third Crusade, *Richard Coeur de Lion* uses the romance genre as a mode of imaginatively shaping English identity in the context of the Hundred Years War.

Finally, we move beyond the tales told about Richard in the Middle Ages to consider how these stories make the transition to modernity. In this regard, the novels of Sir Walter Scott – especially *Ivanhoe* and *The Talisman*, both of which feature Richard as a central character – loom large. It is, for example, the enormous popularity of Scott's novels that plays a pivotal role in connecting

Richard the Lionheart to the Robin Hood tradition, and it is this connection that provides Richard's most enduring literary legacy. Here, Richard's reputation as a crusading king is problematized, particularly in contemporary films, where it becomes a lens through which cultural anxiety about Western wars in the Middle East can be explored.

This book considers Richard I's life and times in the context of the remarkable explosion of literary production that was a hallmark of his late twelfth-century lifetime, and in his long and impressive afterlife in English literature. It seeks to take fiction seriously as an expression of the values that are important to writers and their audiences, as well as how those values change over time. In this regard, the figure of Richard the Lionheart in the literary tradition functions as a screen across which is projected centuries of cultural anxieties and fantasies. Wild stories always circulated around Richard the Lionheart: that he carried King Arthur's sword, that he was a son of the Devil, that he was a cannibal. *Richard the Lionheart* will consider the cultural work these stories performed in their own time and in ours.

ONE

Richard I in the Words
of His Contemporaries

Reflecting on the history of Richard I and his family, the twelfth-century historian Richard of Devizes described them as 'the troubled house of Oedipus'. With this literary allusion, Devizes offers both a rhetorical flourish and an interpretive frame.[1] During his lifetime, chroniclers and historians struggled to bring Richard to life on the page, and in their efforts to do so, they resorted to various rhetorical strategies. For us in the present day, history writing may seem an obvious way to chronicle the past, but medieval history writing does not always adhere to the protocols we expect today. Modern history writing values a deeply researched and unbiased chronological report of the facts of what happened in the past, so far as it is possible to know them. In the Middle Ages, however, history, along with poetry, was an aspect of rhetoric, the art of persuasion. This is not to say that medieval historians thought history writing was somehow false, or designed to mislead. On the contrary, medieval thinkers considered history writing to be a representation of true events, and they often emphasized the importance to the historian's art of eyewitnesses and reliable sources. 'In what I am going to relate I shall, by the help of God, write nothing but what I myself have seen and heard and know to be true, or have on good authority from the testimony or writings of reliable men,' the twelfth-century scholar John of Salisbury wrote in the preamble to his *Historia pontificalis* (Memoirs of the

Papal Court), echoing sentiments common to his contemporaries.[2] Nevertheless, in twelfth-century history writing, rhetorical techniques that are plausible and persuasive are used everywhere, even if they are not strictly, in the modern sense, historical. Thus, for example, long and dramatic speeches are reported verbatim, and characterization is based on classical or biblical precedents. In medieval histories, monastery walls bleed and dragons fly through the night sky as portents of disaster, biblical allusions illuminate the individual's place in the history of salvation, and such classical references as that of Richard of Devizes help the reader to uncover the pattern of human history. History writing was also didactic, and it aimed to provide moral and ethical instruction. 'My aim,' claims John of Salisbury,

> like that of other chroniclers before me, shall be
> to profit my contemporaries and future generations.
> For all these chroniclers have had a single purpose:
> to relate noteworthy matters, so that the invisible
> things of God may be clearly seen by the things that
> are done, and men may by examples of reward or
> punishment be made more zealous in the fear of
> God and pursuit of justice.[3]

England has a long tradition of history writing, beginning in the eighth century with Bede, whose *Ecclesiastical History of the English People* narrates the story of the English from the time of the migration of various Germanic tribes to the island of England to Bede's present day. With the Norman Conquest of England in 1066, however, history writing in England took on a new urgency. Duke William of Normandy invaded and seized control from King Harold Godwinson, who himself had taken the throne when the last Anglo-Saxon king, Edward the Confessor, died without an heir. The Conquest brought a wholesale replacement of England's aristocratic elite, with new lords whose relationship to their new lands was strong militarily, but precarious culturally. This transformed world order required fresh narratives of belonging, and a new generation of historians emerged in response to the crisis. By the twelfth century an efflorescence of narrative history emerges in England that is not seen elsewhere in Europe. These historians sometimes identify themselves as ethnically half-English and half-Norman, and thus uniquely suited to write a new history for a new nation. They draw, in part, on the tradition of history writing inaugurated by Bede, and they tend to begin their histories at the beginning and narrate through to the present of the historian. Alternatively, there is the example of the *History of the Kings of Britain* by Geoffrey of Monmouth (c. 1130s), which takes an entirely different approach, narrating a fictional history of Britain and including – for the first time – the legend of King Arthur. Both styles of history attempt to suture past to present, encompassing both continuity and rupture in the same historical narrative.

By the final decades of the twelfth century, another generation of historians had begun to adopt a different approach. Perhaps for these writers enough time had passed since the Conquest that they were no longer anxious about its meaning for England. Or perhaps the events of their own day – the ascension of Henry II to the throne, putting an end to years of civil war; the inclusion of England in the larger Angevin Empire; the development of an increasingly 'bureaucratic' government during the reign of Henry II; the murder of Thomas Becket, Archbishop of Canterbury; the rebellion of Henry's sons; the crusade and captivity of Richard I; the ascension of King John and the loss of his Continental lands to the French king – were so compelling that they demanded a different method. Certainly, increasingly the men who wrote history were not chiefly monks, but also courtiers and royal administrators. They participated in the events they described and sometimes knew the key players at first hand. Whatever the reason, these historians developed a new focus on contemporary history, and they experimented with a variety of methods. For these reasons, this period has been referred to as the 'golden age of historiography in England'.[4]

This, then, is the context for the historians who took up their quills to record Richard's life and times for posterity. Richard's career was extremely, perhaps uniquely, newsworthy, an impression that seems to have been recognized by his contemporaries. William of Newburgh, for example, described himself as recording 'noteworthy events which have occurred in greater abundance in our day'.[5] Perhaps owing to the novelty of their times and of their task, the historians of Angevin England approached their material from a variety of angles and in a variety of modes. The twentieth-century theorist of history Hayden White notes that, since it is in narrative form, all history writing is necessarily plotted. This is to say that events are ordered in such a way as to produce a story. He further suggests that 'the "emplotment" of history follows one of four generic narratives: romance, tragedy, comedy, and satire'.[6] This is a provocative idea. Without being quite so schematic, it is useful to think of the generic conventions through which twelfth-century historians emplotted their representations of Richard the Lionheart, because the representations of the king that emerge from these histories are therefore, in part, determined by these generic conventions. Conversely, the choice of genre that each historian makes tells us something about his own conception of Richard, and of Richard's place in history. The four historians discussed below – Roger of Howden, Richard of Devizes, Ambroise and Gerald of Wales – although not the only medieval historians by far to treat Richard's life and times, provide an interesting contrast for the differing generic affiliations of their histories. Each writes history in a different mode: chronicle, satire, epic and didactic, respectively. These earliest historical accounts of Richard's life provide a glimpse of a moment when his story was not yet fully crafted, and when the legend of the Lionheart was first coming into being.

The medieval historian whom modern historians trust the most for a faithful and factual account of Richard's career is probably Roger of Howden. 'It is hard to imagine', John Gillingham writes, 'what the reigns of Henry ii and Richard i would look like without the framework provided by his massively detailed chronicles.'[7] Roger was the parson of the minster church of St Peter of Howden in Yorkshire, a position he probably inherited from his father (a practice that was falling out of use during the twelfth century, but which was still not uncommon). He used the title 'magister', or 'master', suggesting that he had spent time studying at a university and was qualified to teach. He put his education to use in the service of not only the Church, but the government; from the early 1170s he was in the service of King Henry ii, accompanying him, for example, to Rome on an

Howden Minster, the benefice of Roger of Howden.

embassy to Pope Alexander in 1171. Throughout the 1180s
Roger appears in various arenas negotiating the king's business.
After the death of Henry II, he seems to have transferred to the
service of the powerful Bishop of Durham, Hugh de Puiset, who
served as one of the Chief Justiciars of England while Richard I
was away on crusade (which is to say that Hugh, along with
William Longchamp, was charged with running England in
Richard's absence). When Longchamp attempted to oust Hugh
from his role and seize power for himself, Roger travelled to France
to bring the scandalous news to King Richard. From there, he
continued in the company of the king as he began his crusade,
travelling first to Sicily, then on to Acre, where he is found wit-
nessing a document in 1191. He subsequently returned to Europe
with the retinue of King Philip of France. It is not entirely clear
how Roger passed the remainder of his life; he may have returned
to his parsonage and lived out his days there, or he may have continued in the service of the bishop or the king. He died in 1202.

This remarkable life spent in royal administration gave Roger
unparalleled access to the important events and actors of his day.
Moreover, this access came at a time when the character of royal
administration itself was changing. Over the course of Henry II's
reign, the financial, judicial and administrative functions of royal
rule were consolidated almost as governmental departments, so
that they were able to function effectively without the personal
oversight, or even the personal presence, of the king. As the historian W. L. Warren describes, Henry II's 'greatest achievement,
indeed, was not that he created a vast dominion, nor even that
he held on to it and largely tamed it, but that he introduced to
it the art of government'.[8] This evolution in royal administration
is evident in Roger's writing. From his vantage point in the royal
administration he wrote a chronicle of his times drawn equally
from his own experience, documentary evidence and court
gossip.

Roger of Howden is the author of a group of interrelated texts.[9] The earliest, titled *Gesta Henrici II et Gesta Regis Ricardi* (The Deeds of Henry II and of King Richard), he began seemingly as a journal of his time at court, and later revised into *Chronica magistri Rogeri de Hoveden* (The Chronicle of Roger of Howden), extending the core years to which he had been witness back to the eighth century and ending with Roger's death in 1202. The chronicle form simply proceeds year by year, describing that year's important events, but offering little by way of emplotment. This is to say that because of the open-ended nature of a chronicle (the years follow one upon another ad infinitum, and Roger's chronicle ends only with his death), the chronicler does not attempt to impose a retrospective meaning on the events he describes; there is no beginning, middle or end to the story. This resistance to the interpretation of events is what, for White, differentiates 'chronicle' from 'history' proper, which narrativizes the raw material, as it were, of the chronicle, restructures it into a story with a plot, and so offers an interpretation of events. White's description here is not at all anachronistic. Medieval writers understood the difference between chronicle and history similarly. Writing at the end of the twelfth century, Gervase of Canterbury noted:

> To some extent the historian and the chronicler have the same goals and use the same material, but their method of handling it is different, as is their form. They share a common purpose, because both strive for truth. The form of their work is different because the historian proceeds in a roundabout and elegant manner, while the chronicler adopts a direct and straightforward course.[10]

The *Chronicle of Roger of Howden*, therefore, is not a first-person account, despite the fact that Roger must have been present at many of the events he describes.

Roger's career gave him access to the documents of administration: correspondence, charters, decrees and so on. What is more, he not only studied these, but also copied them verbatim into his chronicle. In some cases this represents the only surviving copy of the document in question, thus providing inestimable service to the modern historian. Indeed, Roger's innovation in including his documentary sources is part of what attracts scholars to him: it makes him seem modern. By one count, the chronicle transcribes 117 letters, 24 charters and treatises, 10 items of secular legislation and 6 items of ecclesiastical legislation.[11] The inclusion of these documents authenticates the claims Roger makes about the events he describes, and they confer an air of impartiality on the *Chronicle*.[12]

On more than one occasion, Roger includes a letter written by Richard himself, allowing a rare echo of the king's own voice. One of these describes a battle in which Richard obviously feels a more than usual sense of personal pride in his victory over King Philip of France. Having described his assault upon and capture of Courcelles and Gisors, Richard sums up, the king of France

with his forces made a descent in the direction of Gisors, on which, we put him and his people, after taking to flight, into such consternation on their way to the gate of Gisors, that the bridge broke down beneath them, and the king of France, as we have heard say, had to drink of the river, and several knights, about twenty in number were drowned. Three also, with a single lance, we unhorsed, Matthew de Montmoreney, Alan de Ruci and Fulk de Gilerval, and have them as our prisoners. There were also valiantly captured as many as one hundred knights of his, the names of the principal of whom we send to you, and will send those of the rest, when we shall have seen them as Marchadès has taken

as many as thirty whom we have not seen. Men at
arms, also, both horse and foot, were taken, of which
the number is not known; also two hundred chargers
were captured, of which one hundred and forty were
covered with iron armour. Thus we have defeated the
king of France at Gisors; but it is not we who have done
the same, but rather God, and our right, by our means;
and in so doing we have put our life in peril, and our
kingdom, contrary to the advice of all our people.

Richard 1 crowned, while Gisors burns in the background, miniature
from *Grandes chroniques de France*, 1332–50.

These things we signify unto you, that you may share
our joy as to the same.[13]

Despite Roger's lauded impartiality, anecdotes emerge from
the chronicle that give a sense of Richard's personality, as well as
of Roger's opinion of him. It is Roger, for example, who describes
the scene discussed in the Introduction to this book of Philip and
Richard being so close that 'every day they ate at the same table
and from the same dish, and at night had not separate chambers'.[14] One anecdote that conveys a sense of Richard's famous
choleric temper is that of a fight with William des Barres that
spins out of control. In this story, Richard and William (who is,
according to Roger, 'one of the bravest knights in the household
of the king of France') come across a peasant who is transporting
a load of reeds.[15] Richard and William immediately grab a couple
and start horsing around, play fighting. However, when William
breaks Richard's headpiece with his reed, Richard becomes violently angry and attacks him in earnest. When he fails to win the
fight, Richard banishes William, saying, 'Away with you hence,
and take care that you never appear in my presence again, for at
heart I shall for everlasting be the enemy of you and yours.'[16] It
takes the intervention of the king of France, along with 'all the
archbishops, bishops, earls and barons, and chief men of the
army', to reconcile Richard to William. The point of the story
seems to reside in how Richard's temper and intemperateness
risks endangering the cause of the crusade, when it costs good
men. Another anecdote demonstrates not only Richard's temper,
but his sharp wit. A charismatic priest named Fulk, whom Roger
describes as curing the blind and the lame and driving out
devils, comes to Richard and chides him, saying, 'I warn thee, O
king, on behalf of Almighty God, to marry as soon as possible
the three most shameless daughters whom thou hast, lest something worse befall thee.'[17] When Richard replies that he has no

daughters, Fulk reveals himself to have been speaking allegorically, identifying the three daughters as the king's putative sins: pride, avarice and lust. Richard replies quickly and wittily:

> Listen, all of you, to the warning of this hypocrite, who say that I have three most shameless daughters, namely, pride, avarice, and sensuality, and recommends me to get them married: I therefore give my pride to the Knights Templar, my avarice to the monks of the Cistercian order, and my sensuality to the prelates of the churches.

Thus Richard neatly turns the tables on his accuser, implying that if these sins are indeed his, they are shared widely by churchmen. Roger is less impressed, remarking, 'Oh great disgrace, to create a laugh at the expense of the wretched!'[18]

Roger also, however, includes two moments in which Richard repents his sins, both times seemingly sins of the flesh. In the first, while Richard is at Messina preparing to depart on crusade, 'being sensible of the filthiness of his life', he repents and does penance.[19] 'From that hour forward', Roger writes, Richard 'became a man who feared God, and left what was evil and did what was good'.[20] This incident is followed by Richard's meeting with Joachim of Fiore, one of the most famous theologians of the Middle Ages, and one of the most important interpreters of the Book of Revelation, during which Joachim expounded at length his theories about the apocalypse for Richard and his court. This sudden interest in religion seems not to have stuck; several years later, after his return from crusade, Roger describes Richard as being called to repentance once again, this time by a hermit, who admonishes him to be 'mindful of the destruction of Sodom, and abstain from what is unlawful'.[21] It takes a minute, but once again Richard mends his ways, does penance and, 'putting away all illicit intercourse, he remained constant to his wife, and they

Crusaders fighting the dragon of the apocalypse, miniature from
Apocalipsis figurado de los duques de Saboya, 15th century.

two became of one flesh, and the Lord gave him health of both
body and soul.'[22] Roger clearly had hopes for Richard's penitence
that may or may not have been realized.

Roger's final extended description of Richard's life is that
of his death. The account is an elegant rhetorical set piece, complete with reported speech, classical allusions and poetic epitaphs. As Roger tells the story, a certain Guidomar, viscount of
Limoges, has discovered treasure on his lands. He offers a portion
to Richard, but Richard wants it all, so he lays siege to Guidomar's
castle of Châlus. As Richard is surveying the scene of the siege,
he is shot in the arm with an arrow by one Bertram de Gurdun.
The arrow is difficult to extract, and the wound proves mortal.
On his deathbed, Richard forgives Bertram (who, after Richard's
death, is nevertheless flayed alive) most graciously: "'Live on,"
said he, "although thou are unwilling, and by my bounty behold
the light of day. To the conquered faction now let there be bright

hopes, and the example of myself.'"[23] This last quotation, if it does not sound like the Richard we have seen so far, is not – it is borrowed from the Roman epic poet Lucan's *Pharsalia*. Howden ends his description of Richard's life and death with a series of poetic epitaphs, which he ascribes to other writers, including: 'In relation to his death, one writer says: "In this man's death, the lion by the ant was slain."'[24] With this Howden moves on to subsequent events, as all chronicles must.

Such anecdotes are, however, relatively rare in Roger's *Chronicle*, the value of which for modern historians has been in its sober recording of events and its documentary impulse. The chronicle begins before Richard and continues after his death, so that the story is not really about him; he is only one player on the stage. This is in stark contrast to the *Cronicon* (Chronicle) of Richard of Devizes, a work that begins with Richard's coronation and ends with his failure to recapture Jerusalem. It is thus, despite its title, unlike Roger's approach to the chronicle form; it has a beginning, a middle and an end, and it is shaped around the

Château de Châlus-Chabrol, the scene of Richard's death.

main event of Richard's crusade. Writing during the same years as Roger, Devizes nevertheless takes a startlingly different approach to Richard's life. If Roger does not judge, Devizes does not stop judging. The *Cronicon* is history in the mode of satire.

Devizes was a Benedictine monk at St Swithun's, Winchester. The Benedictines were one of the oldest orders of monks, and by the end of the twelfth century the order was international in scope and rich in wealth and influence. St Swithun's, or the 'Old Minster', at Winchester was similarly influential; it had previously been the capital of Alfred the Great's kingdom of Wessex, and it remained an important centre of ceremonial power for the post-Conquest kings of England. It was also a stopping point from the key ports of Portsmouth and Southampton for travellers from all over. So, although a cloistered monk, Devizes was uniquely well placed to gather gossip and information, and gather he did. The *Cronicon* is unique in being a somewhat satirical and gossipy account of the state of the nation in England from the coronation of Richard the Lionheart to the failure of his crusade; it therefore covers only the years between 1189 and 1192, although it is believed that Devizes lived until at least 1198. As its modern translator described the chronicle, 'it combines information with entertainment to a degree not found in any of Richard's [Devizes] contemporaries.'[25]

One of the most interesting things about the *Cronicon* – and rare for medieval texts – is the fact that of the two copies that remain, one seems to have been Devizes's own autograph, working copy. Moreover, the layout of the writing on the manuscript page is unusual, being split between the centre of the page and the margins in such a way that it is not at all clear which, if either, is intended to be 'marginal'. The chronicle begins with the discussion of Richard's reign as the central text, with supplementary events placed, seemingly for added context or colour, in the margins. Once Richard begins his crusade, however, the

Folio from Richard of Devizes, *Cronicon Richardi Divisensis de tempore regis Richardi Primi* (Chronicle of Richard of Devizes of the time of King Richard I), *c.* 1100–1225.

logic shifts, and now events in England occupy the central space, while Richard's escapades in the East take over the margins, at times eclipsing the central narrative.[26] The form of the *Cronicon* thus mirrors its content: the fractured relationship between England and its absent king. The action of the *Cronicon* toggles between Richard's adventures on crusade and the machinations of those left behind, especially Richard's brother John, over the control of the kingdom in his absence.

Almost everything we know about Devizes comes from his own pen, from the dedication at the beginning of the chronicle. Here, he addresses the dedicatee of his work, a fellow monk called Robert, formerly prior of Winchester. Robert has left Winchester to join a new monastic order, the Carthusians, whose style of monasticism was more strictly enclosed than the Benedictines. In a Carthusian monastery, monks lived together, but in isolation. Each monk lived alone, enclosed in his (or her) own cell, leaving it only to attend religious services. Robert had left St Swithun's for Witham Priory, the first Carthusian monastery in England, founded by Henry II in an act of penance for the death of Thomas Becket. The sardonic tone of the chronicle is established in this dedication. Devizes describes wanting to know 'by how much a Carthusian cell is loftier and nearer Heaven than is the cloister at Winchester'.[27] Devizes acquiesces to Robert's request that he should write a chronicle for him with an expression of exaggerated gratitude: 'Oh, how happy I should be if that holy soul, if that angel of the Lord, if that deified man, already counted among the number of the gods, should deign to remember me, who am hardly a man, in his prayers before the great God!'[28] Although Devizes identifies Robert as a friend, he pokes fun at him here in quite a snarky manner. As well as establishing the tone of the chronicle to come, this dedication also suggests that the intended audience of the chronicle is, if not solely Robert, at least a small, select audience of like-minded friends.[29]

The satirical tone and content of Devizes's *Cronicon* are among its most frequently discussed elements; the Victorian editor of the chronicle even described it as 'satire disguised as fact'.[30] Throughout, there is liberal quoting of Latin satirists – Horace, Juvenal, Persius – whom all medieval monks would have encountered in the schoolroom as they learned Latin, but for whom Devizes demonstrates a particular degree of fondness. The highly ironic, satirical and at times sardonic treatment of the material raises the question of interpretation. Who is the intended audience? What is its goal: simply to entertain, or is there a more moralizing intention? In technical literary terms, satire is a subset of irony in that it has a double meaning; what it seems to signify is not what it actually intends. Satire has as its goal the use of irony to single out and to criticize wrongdoing. In this regard, it is strongly moralizing. In the *Cronicon*, however, the moral of the story is often difficult to discern, and frequently the impression is simply that Devizes is amusing himself. We find instances of Devizes's pointed wit throughout, from his comments on Richard the Lionheart's greed ('the king most obligingly unburdened all those whose money was a burden to them') to his description of William Longchamp's physique ('he made up for the shortness of his stature by his arrogance').[31] And he reports King Richard's still scandalous joke: that he would willingly sell London if only he could find a buyer.[32] Nevertheless, the question of how to interpret this tone remains a troubling one, particularly when Devizes describes some of the most important events of his day.

The *Cronicon* opens with a much discussed episode concerning the violence against Jews that accompanied Richard's coronation, and the pogroms that followed in other English towns. 'Winchester alone spared its worms,' Devizes writes of his home city.[33] In its bald antisemitism, this opening is connected to a longer anecdote near the end of the chronicle, describing an abortive ritual murder libel story. 'Because Winchester should not be deprived of its just praise for having kept peace with the Jews, as is told at the beginning of this book,' Devizes begins, before launching into the story of two young Christian French boys who, on the advice of their Jewish employer, travel to England to find better work.[34] Once in Winchester, however, one of the boys disappears, and his friend accuses their Jewish employer of having murdered him: "'This Jew is a devil; this man has torn the heart out of my breast; this man has cut the throat of my only friend, and I presume he has eaten him too.'"[35] Here, Devizes recalls the popular accusation that Jews would kidnap and crucify Christian children in mockery of the crucifixion of Christ.

This story has been the topic of much discussion for its exaggerated rhetoric and sarcastic tone. Is it intended as parody? Is the sarcastic tone Devizes's way of indicating his lack of belief in such accusations and his support of Winchester's Jewish population? If so, why did he previously refer to them as 'worms'? Even more bizarrely, embedded within the story is a satire on the different characters of English towns: Bath and Ely stink, York is full of filthy Scotsmen, Bristol full of soap-makers and London even worse; there 'The number of parasites is infinite. Actors, jesters, smooth-skinned lads, Moors, flatterers, pretty boys, effeminates, pederasts, singing and dancing girls, quacks, belly-dancers, sorceresses, extortioners, night-wanderers, magicians, mimes, beggars, buffoons: all this tribe fill all the houses.'[36] The lengthy diatribe ends with an encomium on Winchester, which is described as perfect in every way:

> That city is a school for those who want to live and
> fare well. There they breed men; there you can have
> plenty of bread and wine for nothing. Monks are there
> of such mercifulness and gentleness, clerks of such
> wisdom and frankness, citizens of such courteousness
> and good faith, women of such beauty and modesty,

that for a little I would go there myself and be a Christian among Christians.[37]

Such great praise ends, however, on an ambivalent note: 'the people of Winchester lie like sentries.'[38] Devizes himself, of course, is from Winchester, and the whole meaning of the story is slippery. The uncertain point of the satire throughout this episode destabilizes our understanding of the meaning.

Devizes's stories of the Jews of Winchester are important because they highlight the difficulty of getting a handle on precisely how he intends his chronicle to be read. Moreover, understanding the thrust of his satire is key to understanding his representation of King Richard. Indeed, his representation of Richard is, it seems, the one place where Devizes lets his satire drop to eulogize the king in the warmest terms. 'And happy', he writes of Richard, 'was this valiant man, because everywhere he found opportunity for bravery.'[39] Almost immediately after his coronation, Richard sets out on crusade:

> The king was indeed worthy of the name of king, for
> in the very first year of his reign, for Christ's sake he left
> the realm of England almost as if he were going away and
> would not return. So great was this man's devotion and
> thus quickly, thus speedily and hastily he ran or, rather,
> flew to avenge Christ's injuries.[40]

When Richard arrives at Acre he is 'received by the besiegers with as much joy as if he had been Christ Himself returning to earth to restore the kingdom of Israel'.[41] Whether this warmth might be read as at times overheated is a tricky question.

At several turns, Devizes takes the opportunity to contrast Richard favourably with his erstwhile frenemy, the French king Philip Augustus. In these anecdotes, Richard consistently outshines the hapless Philip. Thus, for example, Devizes describes Richard's arrival in Messina: 'People of all ages, a crowd beyond number, came to meet the king, marvelling and declaring how much more gloriously and impressively this king landed than did the king of France, who had arrived with his troops a week before.'[42] Philip is similarly eclipsed by Richard's arrival in the Holy Land: 'The king of France had arrived at Acre before Richard and was much thought of by the natives, but when Richard came the king of the French was extinguished and made nameless, even as the moon loses its light at sunrise.'[43] He is subsequently described as the 'paltry king of the French'.[44] In slightly earthier language, Devizes has Safadin, the brother of Saladin, express relief that Philip's uselessness hindered Richard's progress: 'But, thank God, he was burdened with the king of the French and held back by him, like a cat with a hammer tied to its tail.'[45]

It may well be a sign of Devizes's satirical touch that even Safadin has nothing but words of praise for Richard:

> this king, amongst all the princes of the Christian name that the round circle of all the world embraces, alone is worthy of the honour of a leader and the name of a king, for he began his work well, he continued it even better, and, if he remains with you a while longer, he will finish it perfectly.[46]

The final long entry for the chronicle describes the end of Richard's crusade largely through the eyes of Safadin. As the chronicle sets the scene, Richard has now been in the East for two years and the situation is going from bad to worse. He gets no support from his nobles back home. The climate is inhospitable. And then there is the food situation: the French and English soldiers are described as eating everything they can get their hands on, when they can get their hands on it:

The common people among the French and English
feasted together every day in a splendid fashion, no matter
how great the cost, as long as their money held out, and,
with all due respect to the French, they ate till they were
sick. The traditional custom of the English was always
observed, and with proper ceremony they drained their
cups to the sound of clarions and the clangour of trumpets.
The merchants of the province, who brought provisions
to the camp, were astonished at these extraordinary ways
and could scarcely believe what they saw to be true, that
one host of people, and that a small one, should consume
three times as much wine as would sustain several or even
countless hosts of pagans.[47]

Feast is followed by fast, and when the food runs out, the army
is struck with famine. In the midst of these disasters, Richard
falls ill just as Safadin comes to pay him a visit.

In a long and eloquent speech, Safadin describes his love and
respect for Richard, combined with his fear of the English king.
In his speech he offers, in effect, a résumé of Richard's career,
but one based rather in wishful thinking. He describes the fame
of Richard's father in the East, insisting (falsely) that Henry II
'loved this one [that is, Richard] above all his brothers, because
of his uprightness, and chose him rather than his older brothers
to rule over his people'.[48] He (falsely) describes Richard warring
against his elder brothers and expanding his territories in France.
And he recaps many of the events of Richard's crusade that the
chronicle has previously described – the captures of Messina,
Cyprus and Acre – all in the highest form of eulogy. 'Although
we are his rivals,' Devizes has Safadin pronounce, 'we found nothing in Richard to which we could take exception save his bravery,
nothing to hate save his skill at arms.'[49] He imaginatively describes
the Muslims' fear that Richard intends to conquer the whole

world, and their horror at rumours that he 'eats his enemies alive'.[50]

Safadin's speech manages to give the impression that the impending truce between Saladin and Richard is the result of the Muslims' love and respect for Richard, and their unwillingness to attack his armies while he is ill, rather than any military or strategic consideration. Indeed, in what seems to be an attempt to salvage Richard's crusading reputation, Devizes represents the king as wholly unaware of the truce negotiations, which have been conducted behind his back while he is ill. Instead of actively entering into truce negotiations with Saladin, Richard is here represented as acquiescing to the sneaky counsel of his advisors. The chronicle ends with Richard's final refusal to visit Jerusalem: 'the proud swelling of his great heart would not allow him to enjoy as a privilege from the pagans what he could not have as a gift from God.'[51] With these, the final words of the *Cronicon*, the great king is left poised hopelessly in between: in control neither of the kingdom he left behind nor of the kingdom he hoped to gain.

In the *Cronicon*, the satiric mode destabilizes meaning, and nothing can be taken at face value. Although Devizes seems to praise Richard, we are never entirely sure that he is not actually poking fun at the king. The representation of Richard i that emerges, therefore, is of a man slightly diminished, who is not the master of his own destiny, and whose absence from his English kingdom is framed as at least as important as his exploits while on crusade. The exact opposite is the case with a long poem composed at the same time as Devizes was recording his chronicle. Ambroise's *Estoire de la Guerre Sainte* (History of the Holy War), composed in about 1194–5, distinguishes itself from Roger's and Devizes's Latin chronicles in that it was written in French, and it is one of the earliest vernacular histories of the European Middle Ages.[52] With its title of '*Estoire*', 'history', Ambroise announces its generic affiliation with the Latin histories that preceded it, but *estoire* equally translates as 'story', and, indeed, among the most exciting aspects of the *Estoire de la Guerre Sainte* are the moments at which it draws on the French vernacular tradition of epic, *chanson de geste*, in its presentation of Richard the Lionheart as a crusading hero.

About Ambroise himself little is known, except that he was a participant in the Third Crusade, and the *Estoire* is thus significant, like Roger's, as an eyewitness account. On many occasions in the poem Ambroise identifies himself as a witness of the scene, often to express wondrous admiration at the wealth and glamour of it all. He describes a feast rather breathlessly, for example:

> I was present at the feasting in the hall and I saw no
> dirty table-linen, nor wooden chalice or bowl. Rather,
> I saw there rich vessels, embossed, with images cast on
> them, and richly set with precious stones, not in any way
> paltry. I saw there such good service that everyone had
> what he wanted. It was a good and honourable feast as is
> appropriate for such a festival; I have not, it seems to me,
> seen so many rich gifts given at once as King Richard gave
> then, handing over to the king of France and to his people
> vessels of gold and silver.[53]

Within the *Estoire*, Ambroise indicates clearly when he is describing events that he witnessed with his own eyes, and when he is filling in the story with information he has gleaned from elsewhere. This first-person narration gives his story a vivid and lively sense of immediacy. Ambroise, however, does not describe himself as taking part in the fighting, so he was most likely either a cleric or perhaps a jongleur, which is to say an entertainer, one of the many supporting players who typically accompanied elite warriors on crusade.

As we have seen, it is significant that, unlike Roger or Devizes – and the majority of medieval history writing up to the thirteenth century – Ambroise composed his chronicle in the vernacular French. (The interplay between Latin and the vernacular will continue to be important in the tradition of writing about Richard. In the thirteenth century the *Itinerarium Peregrinorum et Gesta Regis Ricardi* translates Ambroise's French into Latin, while *The Crusade and Death of Richard I* translates Roger's Latin into French.[54]) Ambroise's predecessors in vernacular history writing came out of Angevin court circles: Jordan Fantosme's *Chronicle*, which tells the story of the rebellion of Henry II's sons against him from the point of view of politics in the north of England; Wace, whose *Roman de Brut* is a translation of Geoffrey of Monmouth's *History of the Kings of Britain*; and Geoffrey Gaimar, whose *Estoire des Engleis* is a translation into French of the Old English *Anglo-Saxon Chronicle* (among other sources).

In common with these predecessors, Ambroise writes in eight-syllable lines of rhymed couplets.[55] The choice of form and language also signals a different intended audience, no longer primarily the clerical and monastic audience of the Latin prose chronicle; Ambroise is also writing for an aristocratic and courtly audience, knights who had perhaps been on crusade themselves, and their households, and for whom reading about and listening to the heroic deeds of former times were favoured forms of entertainment. Along with the French language, Ambroise appropriates some of the tropes of the Old French epic, or *chanson de geste*. The *chansons de geste* (literally 'songs of deeds') were a popular genre of the late twelfth century (and perhaps had even older, oral antecedents). They tell the heavily fictionalized stories of quasi-historical heroes, such as Alexander the Great and Charlemagne, who must fight to retain their lands and patrimonies, sometimes against a lord who fails to recognize

their true worth, or sometimes against Saracen foes who threaten
their homeland. The most famous of these is *The Song of Roland*,
in which Roland fights on behalf of his uncle Charlemagne with
his friend Oliver against the Muslims in Spain and against his
treacherous stepfather Ganelon, who is in league with them.

The influence of the *chanson de geste* genre on Ambroise's
Estoire de la Guerre Sainte is felt in its frequent gestures to oral
delivery: 'Listen my lords,' Ambroise declaims.[56] The *Estoire* also
frequently references the plots of various *chansons de geste*.
Ambroise compares Guy of Lusignan, erstwhile king of Jerusalem,
to Roland and Oliver – 'Everywhere resounded so to the sound
of his blows that not since Roland and Oliver had there been
such a praiseworthy knight' – and Richard is also compared to
the heroes of *The Song of Roland*.[57] He describes Emperor Isaac of
Cyprus as 'more treacherous and more evil than Judas or Ganelon',
evoking Roland's great enemy.[58] In his description of Messina,
when Richard arrives in Sicily, Ambroise situates the city geogra-
phically, but also reminds his readers that it was once taken by
'Agolant'.[59] Agolant is the antagonist of *The Song of Aspremont*,
a *chanson de geste* that serves as something of a prequel to *The Song
of Roland*; in it Roland, despite being too young to fight when the
African king Agolant invades Italy, nevertheless joins the battle
and comes to the rescue of Charlemagne, along the way capturing
the sword and oliphant (ivory horn) that will become key aspects
of the plot of *The Song of Roland*. Ambroise's representation of
Saladin and Richard's other Muslim antagonists may also reflect
the *chanson de geste* habit of representing Saracens as enemies,
but noble and worthy ones.[60] 'If only he had been a Christian,'
The Song of Roland laments, in its depiction of the noble Saracen,
and similarly Ambroise writes, 'Had they not been infidels no
better people could ever have been seen.'[61]

It is, however, in its representation of Richard 1 through the
lens of the heroes of *chanson de geste* that Ambroise's *Estoire*

Carved ivory oliphant, Fatimid, southern Italy, 11th century.

makes its most significant contribution to Richard's legend. For, although the title of the poem is 'The History of the Holy War', it is really the history of Richard on crusade. The narrative begins with Richard committing to the undertaking – 'Richard, the valiant count of Poitiers, did not wish to fail God at the time of His need and His call. So he took the cross for love of him' – and it ends with Richard's departure from the Holy Land, even while it briefly gestures to the troubles Richard will encounter on his trip home.[62] Richard is characterized as 'shrewd, wise, full of talent', and throughout the poem he is described using epic epithets such as 'valiant', noble', 'courteous', 'wise' and 'generous'.[63] Like Roland, Richard can be reckless, too certain of himself, too eager for glory, but at the same time this recklessness is the other side of the coin of Richard's bravery and chivalry. The description of Richard's army as it marched from Acre would not be out of place in any *chanson de geste*:

> Early in the morning the army mounted and drew up their units. There you would have seen chivalry, the finest of young men, the most worthy and most elite that were ever seen, before then or since. There you would have seen so many confident men, with such fine

armour, such valiant and daring men-at-arms, renowned
for their prowess. There you would have seen so many
pennoncels [streamers] on shining, fine lances; there
you would have seen so many banners, worked in many
designs, fine hauberks and good helmets; there are not so
many of such quality in five kingdoms; there you would
have seen a people on the march who were much to be
feared. King Richard was in the vanguard, with such men
as were not cowards.[64]

In this passage the implicit address to an audience ('there you
would have seen . . .') evokes the oral aspects of early epic, while
the exaggerated glamour of Richard's army suggests the deep
investment in the representation of chivalry of *chanson de geste*.

The influence of *chanson de geste* on Ambroise's representation of the Third Crusade and its heroes, however, should not
be overstated. His poem is an eyewitness account of events in
which he himself participated, and it was intended – and most
likely received – as history writing. Indeed, in one instance he
uses a description of the *chanson de geste* tradition to underline
the truthfulness of the story he is telling:

My lords, I can tell you nothing, of lies or truth, about
the death of Alexander, whose death aroused such
strong feelings, nor of the messenger of Balan, nor of
the adventures of Tristan nor of Paris and Helen who
suffered so much for love, nor of the deeds of Arthur of
Britain and his bold company, nor of Charlemagne and
of Pepin, of Agoland and of Guiteclin, of the old epic
tales of which the jongleurs make so much. I can say
nothing to support or contradict them, nor can I find
anyone to tell me if they are true or false – but of these
which so many saw, and those who suffered themselves

at Acre, of the sufferings they endured, the great heat and the dreadful cold, the injuries and the illnesses – I can tell you of this as truth, and it should be listened to.[65]

In this description of the suffering of the crusaders at the siege of Acre Ambroise contrasts the truthfulness of the story he tells with the uncertain historicity of epic. Of course, the line between epic and history is sometimes difficult to discern. Epic tells stories about historical personages, such as Charlemagne and Alexander the Great, but it does so in a heightened and embellished manner – in the mode of fiction, in other words. It tends to tell stories from the distant past, although the First Crusade proved to be fruitful inspiration for *chanson de geste*, providing the source material and the hero, Godfrey of Bouillon, for the *Chanson d'Antioch* (The Song of Antioch), the *Chanson de Jérusalem* (The Song of Jerusalem) and the *Chanson des Chétifs* (The Song of the Captives). So when Ambroise embarked on his project, the relatively new idea of telling contemporary history in the vernacular, he naturally borrowed from other forms of vernacular literature – and specifically vernacular literature about Christians fighting Muslims. The significance of giving Richard's crusade the vernacular epic treatment is that it puts him on a par with Charlemagne and other famous heroes of antiquity, and in doing so plucks him out of history into the realm of legend. It is also this vernacular epic colouring that first gives Richard his nickname 'Lionheart'.[66]

If Roger of Howden offered history in the mode of chronicle, and Richard of Devizes offered history in the mode of satire, Ambroise's *Estoire de la Guerre Sainte* is perhaps the most influential in the development of the legend of Richard I, casting history in the mode of epic. However, by no means do these three authors exhaust the approaches to writing about the phenomenon that was Richard in the twelfth century. Ralph of Diceto and William

of Newburgh also included Richard's life in their Latin chronicles
(in William's case, alongside several anecdotes about vampires).
Gerald of Wales, who worked as a clerk for Henry II and subsequently for the Archbishop of Canterbury, imagined history in
the didactic mode. A keen observer of the world around him,
Gerald wrote in many genres, including travel narratives and
miracle collections as well as history. His *De principis instructione*
(Instructions for a Ruler) is effectively a two-part work, which
begins with a treatise on the important characteristics that a ruler
should cultivate, including such virtues as patience and modesty,
and illustrated with exemplary stories from history and scrip-
ture. The second part is an account of the end of Henry II's reign,
in which Henry is largely shown to possess few of the virtues
enumerated in the first part of the work. So, although *Instructions
for a Ruler* is not, in the first instance, about Richard, he naturally
plays a role in it, and he is often used as a foil to Henry's character. Gerald is seemingly the first to describe Richard as like a lion,
but it is double-edged praise; Richard is ferocious like the lion but
also, like the lion, prone to sickness:

> Moreover, he who bestowed a nature bestowed also
> the passion of that nature. In order to suppress the most
> ferocious motions of his mind, this our lion, or more
> than lion, is troubled with the pangs of a quartan fever,
> like a lion, because of which he shakes almost continually,
> although he is not disturbed, so much that by his trembling
> he could make the whole world tremble and fear.[67]

Gerald also includes two prophecies of Richard's death. The
first he attributes to a vision of St Godric of Finchale, a contemporary hermit, who sees King Henry and his sons alternately
cleaning a crucifix and defecating on it before throwing it to
the floor and smashing it to bits. The moral of this story, Gerald

tells us, is that although Henry and his sons kept the peace, they persecuted the Church, and for that they will be the victims of divine vengeance. The second prophecy of Richard's end comes as an addendum to his description of the death of King William Rufus – like Richard, killed by an arrow:

> To anticipate something now, to make this clear and point out a certain resemblance of similar things, Count Richard, succeeding his father in the kingdom and being made king, swelled up also in tyrannical pride in his day, and, just as the other suffered an avenging fury from an arrow, so he suffered it from the crossbow, which he used to employ so savagely and so frequently. Hence this verse was composed by someone: 'Christ, the plunderer of your chalice became the booty of Châlus; you cast him down as worthless, who plundered the treasures of the cross'.[68]

Gerald's interest in the exemplary aspects of history writing overwhelms linear chronology, and events and personages are juxtaposed to the best didactic effect.

As the historian Michael Staunton has described: 'All of the historians under discussion, in their different ways, wrote history that was different to anything that had come before.'[69] During Richard i's lifetime, people were moved to record his exploits not simply because of the value of recording current events – an impulse that was fairly new – but because they were aware that there was something extraordinary about him. Overall, it seems clear that framing Richard as a crusading king was important to all those who wrote about him, and this judgement of his contemporaries will continue to influence the literary development of his legend. These historians, writing within Richard's own lifetime, not only strove to capture events truthfully, but attempted to impose meaning on those events. In part, the genre through which they framed Richard's exploits – be it chronicle, satire or epic – is one aspect of this attempt to impose meaning. Sometimes in these histories we seem to learn at least as much about the writers as we do about their subjects. Roger, for example, seems concerned with Richard's (unnamed, undescribed) sexual sins. Devizes, on the other hand, is more concerned with his approach to governance, and with his financial extractions. Ambroise is concerned with recasting the relative failure of Richard's crusade as a success. Rather than obscuring the true nature of historical events, being attentive to the ways in which historians emplot those events brings us closer to a contemporary, medieval understanding of the meaning and import of Richard's reign.

Blondel before Richard's tower, illustration from *Pictures of English History* (1868).

TWO

The Lionheart
and the Troubadours

One of the most enduring legends about Richard the Lionheart is that of the faithful minstrel Blondel. This story is set in the context of Richard's captivity. In 1192 Richard was on his way back from the Middle East by sea, probably not in the best of moods. He had failed in the ultimate goal of retaking Jerusalem, and he was returning to trouble at home. Most of all, he was trying to avoid the French king Philip Augustus, who, since his earlier return from crusade, had been taking advantage of Richard's absence to foment trouble at home. Philip had gained territory from Richard's brother John, who had been manoeuvring to take over Richard's kingdom in his absence. Simultaneously, he had been spreading rumours: especially that Richard had colluded with Saladin. Accused of treason and threatened with arrest, Richard was attempting a route home through the Adriatic, trying to reach the lands of his German brother-in-law Henry the Lion while avoiding Philip's clutches. Unfortunately, a storm forced his ship into port at Venice, and he had no option but to continue his journey over land. This itinerary, however, was equally fraught with danger, since it brought him through the Austrian territories of Duke Leopold v. Leopold held a grudge against Richard: after the siege of Acre, Leopold had planted his banner, hoping to stake a share of the spoils, only to see Richard throw it down and trample it in the mud; he may also have blamed Richard for the assassination of the crusader Conrad of Montferrat, or perhaps it was that Richard had attacked Cyprus on his way east, and taken captive its prince and his wife, relations of Leopold.[1] Whatever the reason, hearing rumours that the king was travelling through his lands, Leopold saw his opportunity for revenge and began to stalk his prey. Attempting to evade capture by disguising himself – as a merchant, a pilgrim or even a kitchen hand, depending on the account – Richard was discovered and captured. After a brief period in Dürnstein Castle as Leopold's prisoner, Richard was sold by Leopold to Emperor Henry VI, who installed him at Trifels Castle.[2]

The events of Richard's captivity alone are further evidence that truth is often stranger than fiction. The narrative of Richard's capture as told by the chroniclers of the twelfth century already had all the elements of a folktale or a romance: the king in disguise

Dürnstein Castle, where Richard was imprisoned.

tpres henry le fecunt regna Richard fun fiz. x. aunze
demy fi entrepayr and de la tere feynt fuft pris del duk
de Ofert par eyde del Roy Phylyppe de fraunce. e fuft reynt hors
de prifon pur cent mil lyueres de argent. e pur cel tauntun fu
rent les chaliz de Englerere pris. des Eglyfes e venduz. Puis
fuft tret de vn quarel de Ablaft al chaftel de Chalezun. dūt
cefte vers fu fet: Xpe tui calicis: predo fit preda calicis.

Richard I shown three times in a miniature from a 13th-century
manuscript: imprisoned in Dürnstein Castle on the left; accompanied
by Mercadier in the centre; and threatened by a bowman at the siege
of Châlus-Chabrol on the right.

as a commoner, evil enemies plotting against him, betrayal by the smallest of forgotten details, the glimmer of a jewelled ring.[3] However, it was only in the thirteenth century that Richard's captivity was embroidered with the story of Blondel the minstrel. This tale stems from an anonymous thirteenth-century satirical history, *Récits d'un Ménestrel de Reims*, or *Stories of a Minstrel from Reims*, an entertaining take on recent history, leaning towards the satirical and the salacious. The story concerns Blondel, a young minstrel who, having been raised by Richard, decides to go looking for the captive king. He travels for a year and a half, until one day:

> By chance he entered Austria and came directly to
> the castle in which the king was being held prisoner.
> He stayed with a widow, and asked her to whom the
> fine, strong, well-situated castle belonged, and she
> replied that it belonged to the duke of Austria. 'Lovely
> hostess,' Blondel said, 'are there any prisoners in the
> castle?' 'Yes,' she said, 'there is one, who has been there
> for four years, but we do not know who he is. I tell you
> they certainly guard him well and carefully; we believe
> that he is a gentleman and a great lord.'[4]

So Blondel seeks employment at the castle and is hired as a jongleur. He remains at the castle over the winter, never discovering the identity of the prisoner, until:

> One day, during Easter, while he was walking alone
> in the garden near the tower, Blondel looked around
> him, thinking that he might, by chance, see the
> prisoner. As he was doing this, the king looked through
> an archer's slot, and saw Blondel. He thought about
> how to make him recognize him, and he remembered

a song that they had made up together, which only the
two of them knew.

He began to sing the opening words loudly and clearly,
for he sang very well, and when Blondel heard him, he
knew certainly that this was his lord. In his heart he felt
greater joy than he had ever felt, and he left the garden,
and went to his room, where he reclined, picked up his
Vielle, and began to play, singing of his joy at having
found his lord.[5]

Blondel subsequently returns home to England, where he is able
to alert the English barons to the king's whereabouts. Delighted,
the barons send messengers to Austria with a large ransom, and
the king is rescued. In yet another hundred years' time the story
is further refined so that it becomes Blondel whose singing is
overheard and recognized by the captive king. This is the version of the story subsequently learned by generations of English
schoolchildren.

Although the legend of Richard and Blondel is not historical, it nevertheless draws strength from the efflorescence of
literary culture in the second half of the twelfth century, and
from Richard's connection to it.[6] Richard I was one of the first
kings of England to pay attention to his representation in the
arts. He surrounded himself with poets in the hope that they
would commemorate him, even – or perhaps especially – on
crusade. Legend has it that he enjoyed poetry and music so much
that he requested a Muslim musician from Saladin's brother and
enjoyed the performance very much. These were the decades that
brought an explosion of imaginative literature in the French
language; the first romances, *chansons de geste*, vernacular saints'
lives and histories all date from these years. The earliest of these
vernacular literary traditions was troubadour poetry. It was precisely during the years of Richard's reign that this genre reached

Minstrels with a rebec and a lute, miniature from *Cantigas de Santa María – Códice de los músicos*, 13th century.

its apogee, and Richard is a frequent subject of troubadour verse. The troubadours Marcabrun, Bernart de Ventadorn, Peire Vidal, Bertran de Born, Guiraut de Borneil and Raimbaut de Vaqueiras wrote both for Richard and about him, and through their poems we gain insight into the perception of Richard by his contemporaries. Moreover, in these poems about Richard we see reflected the development of two of the most important topics of troubadour poetry: love and politics. Indeed, there are two poems attributed to Richard himself: the prison lament 'Ja nus hons pris' ('No prisoner will speak his mind') and the political *sirventes* 'Dalfin je us voill desrenier' ('Dalfi, I want to clear up a few things').

We know of some 400 troubadours who left us 2,500 poems, in a tradition that lasted for approximately 250 years, from the

beginning of the twelfth century to the beginning of the fourteenth. The earliest troubadour poetry seems to have been centred
on the court of Poitou, of which Richard would become count.
The troubadours were men and women from a variety of social
classes, from nobility to simple clerics. What they have in common
is the language of their poetry – Occitan, the language of the
region that is now the South of France – and its themes.[7] 'Poetry'
is perhaps not quite the correct term, in fact, since these lyrics
were first and foremost songs. Musical notation survives, and
some were transmitted orally for a century before being written
down and collected into songbooks, or *chansonniers*, in the thirteenth century. At that time the poems themselves were joined
in the manuscripts by anonymously written *vidas*, or biographies
of the troubadours, and *razos*, supplementary prose introduc-
tions to or explanations of the poems, which serve to elucidate
the context and plot of the allegorical and allusive poetry.

The poetry of the troubadours is, for the first time since classical antiquity, secular in orientation. It is directed at life in this
world, not in the next, and is orientated on the courts of the
aristocracy of southern France. It thus reflects their concerns:
power and politics, chivalry and games, but also love. The key values of troubadour poetry are joy, youth, courtesy and generosity,
and they share a strong aesthetic. Perhaps the most enduring
legacy of troubadour poetry is the theme of courtly love or *fin'amor*,
as it was referred to by the troubadours. *Fin'amor* describes a
refined and true love with strong erotic elements. It is the love
the troubadour addresses to an absent or unattainable lover, the
amor de lonh, 'love from afar'. It is sometimes adulterous, but not
always, and mostly in fantasy rather than fact. The love object is
usually addressed by a pseudonym, a *senhal*, and remains anonymous to the audience. The fulfilment of the love affair would
elevate both lover and beloved, but its goal is more often ful-
filled in its poetic expression. Many scholars have noted that the

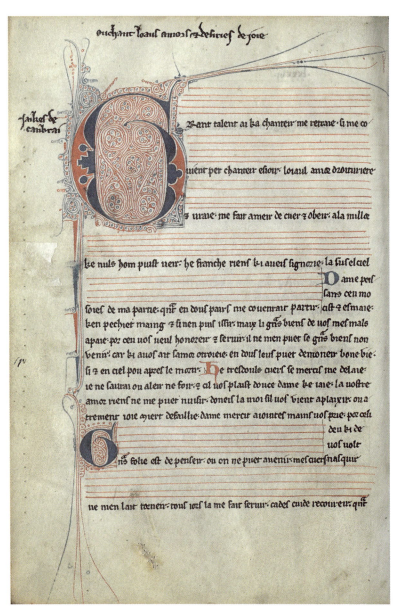

ouchant loiaul amors z deliries de ioie

chiuof de cambrai

ant talent ai ba chanteir me retraie. si me co
uient per chanteir estoir. loiaul amor droituriere
urare. me fait ameir de cuer z obeir. ala milla
be nuls hom puist veir. he franche riens li auers signozie. la suf el ciel
Dame poi
sans ceu mo
soiez de ma partie. qut en dous pars me couenrair partir. ast z esmaie.
ben pechiet maing. z si nen puis istir. mais li gns biens de uos mes mals
apaie. por ceu uos neul honozeir z seruir. il ne men puet se gns biens non
venir. car li auos ait samos otroieie. en dous leus puet demoneir bone bie.
si z en ciel pou aptel le morir. he tresdous cuers se merci me delaie.
ie ne saurai ou aleir ne foir. al uos plaust donce dame be iaie. la uostre
amor riens ne me puet nuisir. doneis la moi sil uos vient aplaixir. ou a
trement ioie ayiert defaillie. dame merci aiointes mains uos prie. por cou
deu li de
uos uolt
gns folie est de penseir. ou on ne puet auenir. mes cuers nasquir
ne men lait traenir. tous ieis la me fait seruir. cades cuide recouvreir. qut

elevation of the courtly lady, and of women in general, is more to do with rhetoric than reality.

The poetry of the troubadours, however, was not limited to love songs (*cansos*). Other genres include the *planh*, a song of lament; the *tenso*, or debate poem; and the *sirventes*, a moralizing satirical or political song.[8] Indeed, only about half of the surviving troubadour lyrics are love poems. In this genre directed at an elite audience with elite themes, it is perhaps not surprising that political poems were as popular as love poems and sought to intervene in various military and political struggles. In this regard we might think of the genre of the *sirventes* as a form of soft power. Richard himself was the author of two *sirventes*.

It was during Richard's reign – first as duke of Aquitaine and then as king of England – that the tradition of troubadour poetry reached its apogee. His connection with this literary culture is hereditary; his maternal great-grandfather, William, VII count of Poitiers and IX duke of Aquitaine (1071–1127), is counted as the first troubadour. The twelfth-century historian Orderic

William IX of Aquitaine, troubadour and Eleanor of Aquitaine's grandfather, historiated initial from a *Chansonnier provençal* manuscript, 13th century.

Vitalis describes William entertaining others with songs about his experiences on crusade, writing that he 'often related the miseries of his captivity in the presence of kings and magnates and groups of Christians, using rhythmical verses with elegant modulations'.[9] His poems describe love and sex, as well as his own experiences of war. They range from the romantic ('No man will ever really be refined/ With respect to love, if he is not submissive to it') to the downright filthy ('I do not like a guarded cunt nor a fishing hole without fish').[10] Very often, as with all great poets, his poems are about poetry itself: 'I will make a verse out of nothing,' he proclaimed in one of his most famous poems.[11] He did more than that, inaugurating a genre that would achieve its highest attainment during the reign of his great-grandson. The most celebrated troubadour poets flourished during the second half of the twelfth century: Marcabrun (1140–1185), Bernard de Ventadour (c. 1148–1195), Peire Vidal (1175–c. 1215), Bertran de Born (c. 1140–1212/15), Guiraut de Borneil (c. 1138–1215), Raimbaut de Vaqueiras (fl. 1180–1207) and Gaucelm Faidit (fl. 1172–1203). Richard was a patron of the arts and also a favourite subject of the poets; as one of the most famous and charismatic figures of his age it could hardly be otherwise.

There is, for example, a charming anecdote in the razo to a poem by Arnaut Daniel that describes Richard presiding over a poetry competition at his court:

> And it happened that he [Arnaut Daniel] was in the
> court of King Richard of England and, while at that
> court, another joglar provoked him, saying that he
> composed in richer rhymes than he (Arnaut). Ar(naut)
> took offence with this and, with the King's power as
> guarantor, they made a bet, each betting his saddle
> horse that the other couldn't do as well as he could.
> The king locked each of them in a room. Sir Ar(naut),

due to the indignation that he felt, was unable to link one word with another. The joglar composed his song quickly and with ease. They had been given only ten days, and in just five days they were to be judged by the King. The joglar asked Ar(naut) if he had composed his song and Ar(naut) said yes, that he had finished his song three days earlier, when in fact he had not even thought about it. The joglar sang his song all night so that he would be sure to know it well. Sir Ar(naut) thought of a way to pull a joke on him. One night while the joglar was singing, Sir Ar(naut) went and memorized the song and the melody. When they went before the King, Sir Ar(naut) said that he wanted to perform his song, and he began to sing beautifully the song that the joglar had composed. And the joglar, when he heard it, looked him in the face and said that it was he who had composed it. The King asked how that could be, and the joglar begged the King to find out the truth; so the King asked Ar(naut) how this had come about. Sir Ar(naut) told him what had happened and the King was greatly amused and took it all as a great joke. The bets were called off and he had fine gifts given to each of them.[12]

This anecdote demonstrates Richard actively engaging with the production and enjoyment of troubadour poetry at court. But this was more than a poetry of leisure, and troubadours also played a role in Richard's crusading. Folquet de Marseille uses song to encourage Richard to go on crusade ('Chantars mi torn ad afan'). Guiraut de Borneil similarly addressed poems to Richard, before following him to the Holy Land. Peire Vidal, who also accompanied Richard on crusade, references Richard's role in the politics of the time in several lyrics. One poem in particular addresses Richard twice. First Vidal complains of not having been paid for his services, then he concludes: 'Count of Poitou, my lord, you and I/ have received the whole world's praises:/ you for doing and I for speaking well.'[13]

The most memorable of the troubadours who fêted Richard was Bertran de Born, who variously immortalizes Richard, his father and his brothers in his poems across the course of his long career. Lest we think of troubadours as solely poets of love, Bertran was most certainly also a poet of war. 'War pleases me, though love and my lady make war on me all year long, for I see courts and gifts and pleasure and song all enhanced by war,' he announces memorably in 'Gerr'e trebailh vei et afan'.[14] In one of his most famous poems he brings together the poetic trope of springtime, when a young man's heart should turn to love, and his favourite topic of war:

> The gay time of spring pleases me well, when leaves and
> flowers come; it pleases me when I hear the merriment
> of the birds making their song right through the wood;
> it pleases me when I see tents and pavilions pitched
> on the meadows; and I feel great happiness, when
> I see ranged on the fields knights and horses in armour.[15]

The thirteenth-century *vida* that prefaces his poems in the *chansonniers* describes him thus:

> Bertran de Born was a castellan from the bishopric of
> Perigord, and he was the lord of a castle called Hautefort.
> He was at war with his neighbors all the time, with the
> count of Perigord, and with the viscount of Limoges, and
> with his brother Constantine, and with Richard as long as
> he was count of Poitiers. He was a good knight and a good
> warrior, and a good lover of ladies, and a good inventor of
> poetry, and he was wise and eloquent, and he knew well

how to deal with good and with evil men. He influenced, whenever he wished, King Nery and his son; but he always wanted them to be at war with one another, the father, the son, and the brother, one against the other. And he always wanted the king of France and the king of England to be at war with each other. And if they had a peace or a truce, he would at once make an effort with his *sirventes* to underdo the peace, and to show how each one of them was being dishonored by that peace. And thus he reaped much gain and much loss.[16]

We find Bertran in the ambit of Richard the Lionheart beginning in the autumn of 1182, at Argentan in Normandy, where Henry II assembled his Christmas court to celebrate the arrival of his daughter Matilda and son-in-law Henry the Lion of Saxony. Bertran addressed two poems to Matilda under the sobriquet 'Helen', evoking the heroine of Troy, who was no doubt well known at the Plantagenet court from the recent *Roman de Troie* (The Romance of Troy) by Benoît de Sainte-Maure, itself addressed to Matilda's mother, Eleanor of Aquitaine. These poems embody the classic tropes of troubadour love poetry: 'She is of such a loving look that I'll die if she doesn't regale me with a sweet kiss.'[17] The poems written on the occasion of the Christmas court at Argentan are important because they attest to the presence of Occitan poetry in Plantagenet circles. They also offer Bertran's tongue-in-cheek assessment of the atmosphere at Henry II's court: 'A court is never complete without joking and laughter; a court without gifts is a mere mockery of barons! And the boredom and vulgarity of Argentan nearly killed me, but the noble, lovable body and sweet, mild face and good companionship and conversation of the Saxon lady protected me.'[18]

Subsequently, however, Bertran found even more compelling subject matter in the rebellion of the Aquitanian barons against

Richard, then duke of Aquitaine. The origin of the crisis seems
to have been in Richard's intervention in a disputed inheritance
of the county of Angoulême, but the barons may also have been
restless under his rule and resented his attempts to assert control
over the region. One English chronicler records that as duke
Richard 'oppressed his subjects with unjustified demands and a
regime of violence'. Another reports, somewhat more sensation-
ally, that he was stealing the counts' wives and making them his
concubines.[19] When Henry II attempted to appease his eldest son,
the 'Young King' Henry, by having his younger brothers do him
homage, the Young King was awkwardly forced to admit that he
could not accept Richard's homage because he had made prom-
ises to support the rebel barons against him. By 1183 war had
broken out between Richard and the Young King, who had taken
the side of the rebels against his brother, as had their younger
brother Geoffrey. Bertran de Born was the great propagandist of
this conflict, and he was firmly on the side of the rebels.

No fewer than fourteen of Bertran's poems fan the flames
of this war. In a poem of 1182, Bertran suggests that Richard's
building of a new castle at Clairvaux is a deliberate provocation
to the Young King: 'at Clairvaux they have built a beautiful castle
without a by-your-leave and put it in a flat field. I don't want
the Young King to know it or see it, because he would not like
it.'[20] In the same poem he calls out the chief barons one by one,
reminding them of their grievances, praising the brave and
soliciting others to the cause:

> If the mighty viscount, who is head of the Gascons and
> whom Béarn and Gavardan obey, and Sir Vezian want
> it . . . then Richard will have plenty to do down this
> way; nevertheless, since he is valiant, let him climb
> up here with the great army he's drawing together.[21]

When, in 1183, it seemed as though the younger Henry were hoping to make peace between Richard and the barons, Bertran reacted angrily:

> I won't put off a sirventes any longer, such an urge I have
> to speak up and spread the strange news; I have a great
> story about the Young King, who has dropped his claim
> on his brother Richard, because his father told him to.
> He says he was driven to it! Since Sir Henry neither
> holds nor governs land, let him be King of the Fools![22]

With these *sirventes*, Bertran earned himself a place in Dante's *Inferno*, doomed to carry his severed head in his hands: 'I am Bertran de Born,' he announces, 'the one who gave bad counsel to the fledgling king. I made the son and father enemies: . . . Because I severed those thus joined, I carry – alas – my brain dissevered from its source, which is within my trunk.'[23]

Ultimately, Henry II was forced to intervene on Richard's behalf, in order to get his sons under control and to assert his dominance over his eldest son, who chafed at his position of relative powerlessness in relation to his brothers, forced as he was to wait longer than them for his inheritance. However, tragedy struck. The Young King fell ill with a fever and died. His death left his father and Bertran grief-stricken, and Richard heir to the kingdom. Bertran wrote a famous lament for the Young King:

> Forevermore I close my song in grief and suffering and
> think it ended, for I have lost my subject and my joy and
> the best king ever of a mother born – generous and well
> spoken, and a good horseman, handsome, and humble in
> conferring great honours. I fear that grief torments me so
> much that it will choke me, for I talk about it unceasingly.[24]

With his father's help Richard ultimately crushed the baronial rebellion, and in July 1183 he seized Bertran's castle, Hautefort. Bertran rather diplomatically attempted to put a good face on things: 'I am not so downcast, even though I have lost, that I don't sing and have fun and scheme to recover Autafort.'[25] Henry did, in fact, return Hautefort to Bertran. A *vida* by Bertran offers an apocryphal but charming anecdote:

> And Bertran de Born used to boast that he was of
> such worth that he did not think he would ever
> need all his wit. And afterwards the King took him
> prisoner, and after he had imprisoned him, he said
> to him, 'Bertran, you will now need all of your wit.'
> And Bertran answered that he had lost all his wit
> when the Young King died. So the king wept for
> the death of his son and pardoned him and gave
> him clothing and land and honour.[26]

Bertran henceforth switched sides and threw his political and literary support behind Henry and Richard. He writes of Richard: 'If the count is generous to me and not stingy, I'll be very valuable to him in his affairs, and true as a piece of silver, trusty and bright.'[27] In the *sirventes* of this era, Bertran gives Richard the much-debated nickname 'Oc-e-No' – 'Yes and No' – perhaps because of his changing humour or for his quick and sudden decisions.[28] For example, Bertran now encourages Richard against the rebel barons:

> A man without a lady cannot make a love song, but I'll
> compose a fresh sirventes, fresh and new. Since our barons
> dream of punishing the lord of Bordeaux with war and
> making him affable and courteous by force, he should be
> so rude to them that each would be overjoyed at a word

from him; they shouldn't be annoyed if he flays and shears them.[29]

And he celebrates Richard's return from his German captivity in his own inimitable style:

> Now comes the charming season when our ships will reach the shore, and the king will come gallant and worthy. King Richard has never been so great before! Then we shall see gold and silver spent, catapults shot and discharged, walls tumbled, towers toppled and dropped, and enemies chained and captured.[30]

For Bertran, Richard is the ultimate provocation to song:

> When I see banners yellow, violet, and blue unfurled among the orchards, the neighing of the horses soothes me, and the songs the minstrels sing as they go fiddling from tent to tent, and the trumpets and horns and clarions clear; then I want to compose a sirventes for Count Richard to hear.[31]

Richard the Lionheart, then, participated in a culture in which poetry and song were an important aspect of both private and public life. Troubadours and jongleurs, or minstrels, travelled from court to court, and as they did so they spread gossip and news alongside, or even in the form of, literary compositions. They were entertainers, but also propagandists. For his part Richard clearly served as a protector and patron of troubadours, as well as a subject of their verses. Most interesting, however, is that he participated in this literary culture not only as patron but as poet. His earliest poem, unfortunately, has not survived. Evidently while on crusade the decision not to attempt an attack

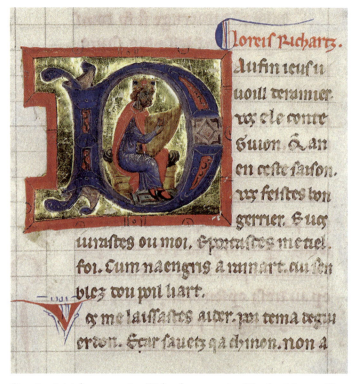

Opening initial representing Richard I composing 'Daufin, je'us vuoill derainier', from a *Chansonnier* manuscript, 13th–14th century.

on Jerusalem caused widespread consternation within the army. In this context Ambroise's *Estoire de la Guerre Sainte* tells us that the duke of Burgundy composed a mean song about Richard. 'What could the king do but reciprocate with a song about those who worked against him and mocked him through envy?' asks Ambroise, rhetorically.[32]

Happily, however, two poems by Richard have survived. Both are topical songs, interventions in the politics of the moment. The first, 'Ja nus hons pris', survives in ten manuscripts and with its musical notation in four. This is a remarkable survival rate, and it is most likely thanks to Richard's fame, as well as the infamy of his imprisonment.[33] Addressed nominally to his half-sister Marie de Champagne, it obliquely targets all his vassals, complaining about their sluggishness in obtaining the money for his release.

'Ja nus hons pris'

I.

No prisoner will speak his mind fittingly unless he does so as a man in sorrow; but he can, for consolation, make a song. I have friends enough but the gifts are few; they will be shamed if for want of my ransom I am here for two winters a prisoner.

II.

This my men and my barons – English, Norman, Poitevin, and Gascon – know full well: I never had a companion so poor I would leave him in prison for the sake of wealth. I do not say this as a reproach, but I am still a prisoner.

III.

Now I well and truly know for certain that a dead man or prisoner has no friend or family, since I am left here for the sake of gold or silver. I fear for myself, but even more so for my people, for after my death they will be dishonoured, if I am held prisoner for a long time.

IV.

It is no wonder I have a grieving heart when my lord causes havoc in my land. If he were to remember our oath which we both made together, I know for sure that I would no longer be a prisoner here.

V.

The men of Anjou and Touraine, those youths who are free and healthy, know full well that I am held far from them in another's hands; they would help me greatly but see no money coming. The plains are now empty of fine arms because I am a prisoner.

VI.

My companions whom I loved and love still – the lords
of Cayeux and of Perche – tell them, song, that they
are not men to rely on: the heart I had for them was
never false nor faltering. If they now wage war on me,
they will act most basely, as long as I were to remain
a prisoner.

VII.

Countess sister, may the one to whom I appeal and on
whose account I am a prisoner save and guard your
sovereign worth for you.

VIII.

I do not say this about the one in Chartres, the mother
of Louis.[34]

This song is often described as a *rotrouenge* in form (which is to
say, short stanzas usually of ten syllables, sharing a single rhyme
sound). It was composed in Old French, not the Occitan typical of troubadour song, but it also exists in an Occitan version,
so that technically Richard is not a troubadour, but a *trouvère*,
the corresponding term for the lyric poets of northern France.
Some scholars have suggested that Richard himself might have
translated it from French to Occitan, although it is perhaps more
likely that the language was adapted by others for Occitan
songbooks.[35]

It opens with the suggestion that the poet is a metaphorical
prisoner of love, but by the end of the first stanza it is clear that
his prison is literal and that he awaits ransom. Each stanza ends
with a shorter line and all end on the same word, *pris*, prison,
driving home the theme of the poem. The poem thus overturns
the conventions of the typical troubadour lyric; instead of being
a prisoner of love, the poet is a political prisoner, and instead of
being abandoned by a lover he feels abandoned by his vassals.

Across the stanzas that follow he addresses all those who he feels should be helping him: the men of his dominions, England, Normandy, Poitou, Gascony, Anjou and Touraine. He addresses them as beloved friends and companions, but implies that they value money over friendship. And he expresses his dismay that others are harassing his lands when he is in no position to defend them, but can survey his kingdom only in verse. In the fourth stanza he addresses his complaints to the king of France, Philip Augustus, with whom he swore an oath that they would not trouble each other's lands while they were on crusade. Philip did not live up to this promise during Richard's imprisonment, and he cultivated Richard's youngest brother, John, who was himself attempting to take over Richard's domains. The final two stanzas turn to his two half-sisters, daughters of Eleanor of Aquitaine and Louis VII of France: Marie de Champagne, whom he addresses in warm terms; and Alix de Blois, whom he does not. The final stanza takes aim at Alix's son Louis, who Richard feels has betrayed him by siding with his enemies during his absence. A tone of disappointment and frustration emerges clearly from this poem. Its short stanzas and simple rhyme scheme lend it a quiet power, while the repetition of 'prisoner' expresses a barely concealed undercurrent of fury. Here, unable to wage the literal war at which he was famously effective, Richard wages an ideological war, aiming at the hearts and minds of his subjects.

The second of Richard's poems, written after his release from captivity, has a similar political theme. 'Daufin, je'us vuoill derainier' (Dalfi, I want to clear up a few things) is an Old French *sirventes* addressed to the Dauphin d'Auvergne, which was answered in similar style by the Dauphin with a poetic response in Occitan. Dalfi d'Auvergne and his cousin Guy were lords of the county of Auvergne and vassals of Richard in his role as duke of Aquitaine. Formerly supporters of Richard in his continual struggles with Philip Augustus, they felt abandoned by Richard when in 1195 he contracted with Philip a short-lived peace treaty that ceded Richard's rights over Auvergne to the French king. Dalfi, therefore, refused to offer Richard any help when the peace broke down and his war with Philip recommenced. Richard responded with the following *sirventes*:

1. Dalfi, I want to clear up a few things
With you and Count Guion,
For during this year
You were good fighters
And swore allegiance to me;
And you had such faith in me,
Like Sir Aengris had in Rainart.
Now you seem like two grey hens.

2. You gave up helping me
Over the manifestation of a reward
And because you knew that
There was no money or riches in Chinon.
You want a rich king,
Good at arms, who keeps his word,
And since I'm a cheap coward,
You turn around and support the other side.

3. I still want to ask you
About Issoire: whether it's all right with you,
Or if you're going to take vengeance
And go hire mercenaries.
But there's one thing I'll assure you of:
If you were to break the law
You would find in Richard
An excellent warrior for the banner of his land.

4. In the beginning I saw you
As generous, living in a great home.
Then you found a reason
To erect a fortified castle
And you gave up on gifts and pleasure,
Holding court and going to tournaments.
But reputation doesn't matter
When Frenchmen are like Lombards.

5. Go *sirventes*, I am sending you
To Auvergne;
And tell the two counts for me
That if from now on they cause any trouble, God
help them!

6. Why sing when a valet betrays his word
And a servant boy respects no law?
But from now on, each of them had better watch
his step
Or he'll get the worst of it as his share.[36]

In the poem Richard recalls Dalfi's former loyalty, comparing
their relationship to the fox (Rainart) and wolf (Sir Aengris/
Isengrin) fables of Reynard (Renart/Renard) the Fox. Here the
wolfish Isengrin is a symbol for treachery and betrayal. He suggests that money rather than honour and loyalty is the motiva-
tion for Dalfi's behaviour, comparing Dalfi to a 'Lombard', when
Lombards had the reputation of being prosperous but also of
practising usury. He taunts Dalfi for the loss of Issoire, which
Philip had seized. The accusation here is a serious one; Richard
accuses Dalfi not simply of failing to come to his aid, but of be-
traying the basic principles of courtliness: honour, loyalty and
generosity. For his part Dalfi responds with a pointed riposte in

Occitan, 'Reis pus vos de mi chantaz'. The strophes of this song cleverly repeat the structure of Richard's. Dalfi pushes back at Richard's accusations, suggesting that a king 'whom the wicked Turks/ Feared more than a lion' ought to have been able to protect his territories at home, and accusing Richard of 'leaving him in the lurch'. 'If you didn't seem so fickle,' Dalfi protests, 'I would have returned to you.'[37] Nevertheless, the poem ends with the promise of a rapprochement between the two men.

These two poems of Richard the Lionheart seem to give us a glimpse into Richard's personality. They are the products of skilful rhetoric, to be sure, but they show him deploying the values of courtliness and loyalty as a mode of persuasion alongside military might. They also highlight the extent to which, in the second half of the twelfth century, the writing of public poetry was an important aspect of political culture. It was at this time that vernacular political song emerged as a minor yet significant literary genre.[38] Still, they remain poems, not news dispatches. Although they seek to intervene in a crisis of the moment, they do so in a way that is designed to produce an emotional, as much as a political, response. Richard's poetry is as interested in making an aesthetic statement as it is in making a political one, and it brings together the two aspects of medieval kingship at which Richard excelled: war and courtly culture.

If Richard provided endless inspiration to the troubadours in life, so it was in death. It was precisely this sense of Richard as the very incarnation of chivalry that the troubadour Gaucelm Faidit mourned in the moving lament he composed when Richard died in 1199. 'Fortz Chausa es', the lament begins:

It is very cruel that it should fall to me to tell and recapitulate in song the greatest unhappiness and greatest grief that I, alas, have ever experienced, and that I must now, weeping, lament . . . For he who was head and father of Valour, the mighty and valiant Richard, King of the English, is dead. Alas! Oh God! What a loss and what a blow! What a cruel world, and what a hard word to hear.[39]

The lament dwells equally on the poet's grief and on Richard's accomplishments: his bravery, generosity and nobility. He is compared to Alexander the Great, to Charlemagne and to King Arthur. 'Alas, valiant lord king,' the poet asks, 'what will happen now to arms and to the rough and tumble of tournaments, to rich courts and fine gifts, since you will no longer be there?'[40] His like, Gaucelm laments, will not soon be seen again. The words and music for the first two verses of this lament are inscribed in a manuscript following the only surviving copy of Ambroise's *Estoire de la Guerre Sainte*. It thus completes that epic narrative of Richard's life, concluding with the end of his crusade, and with a fittingly heroic lament on his death.[41]

Richard's lifetime tracked the height of troubadour poetry in the second half of the twelfth century, and in retrospect the two appear to be deeply imbricated. Richard provided a larger-than-life persona that connected naturally with the themes dear to the troubadours: youth, courtliness, loyalty, generosity, prowess. Meanwhile, the poetry of the troubadours provided him with an arena for the expression of his own sense of courtliness, and with a locus of diplomacy and political persuasion outside the field of battle. The themes first fully articulated in troubadour poetry – especially that of the ennobling nature of romantic love – set the tone for the literary culture of the entire medieval period. Today, troubadour lyric is widely seen as significant for the insight it gives us into medieval social history, particularly the history of gender; into the social world of the feudal nobility of all ranks; and into the development of literature in the European vernacular languages.[42] Considering the engagement of

Richard with the culture of troubadour lyric also allows us to watch the development of, and even the curation of, his legend during his own lifetime.

THREE

Romancing Richard the Lionheart

O nly slightly more than a hundred years after Richard's death, his celebrity – and notoriety – was confirmed when he returned as the hero of romance. The Middle English romance that preserves his legend, *Richard Coeur de Lion*, loosely follows the real-life adventures of Richard I on the Third Crusade, but embellishes them with the tropes of romance. It was extraordinarily unusual in the Middle Ages for a relatively contemporary figure to receive this treatment; heroes of romance, when historical, tended to be from the distant past, such as Alexander the Great and Charlemagne, or from the realms of myth, such as King Arthur and Sir Gawain. *Richard Coeur de Lion* intersperses a quasi-historical narrative of Richard's adventures on the Third Crusade with a series of fantastical episodes that embroider his life story and which offer a glimpse into the cultural work that the figure of Richard was doing in the later Middle Ages. Such fantastical episodes include the representation of Richard as the son of a fairy (or demon) mother, and as a cannibal king who both feasts on his Muslim enemies and serves them for dinner. In this regard *Richard Coeur de Lion* itself embodies its portrayal of Richard: bold, feisty, uncouth and a bit strange.

Although Richard was already renowned in his own time, this popular romance, which circulated for two hundred years in manuscripts and was twice printed in the sixteenth century, fully established the king as a figure of legend. Furthermore, in its representations of Richard's crusading allies, the French king Philip Augustus and his knights, as fickle and treacherous – to the point where the negative representation of French allies exceeds that of Muslim enemies – it established Richard, whose real-life identity seems to have been largely French, as an emphatically *English* king. In this regard *Richard Coeur de Lion*, although set during Richard's battles with Saladin for control of Jerusalem during the Third Crusade, is deeply invested in shaping English national identity in the context of the Hundred Years War, which was ongoing during the late fourteenth/early fifteenth-century era of the romance's composition and circulation. Moreover, as with Richard's celebration in troubadour verse, *Richard Coeur de Lion* demonstrates how the figure of Richard the Lionheart is entangled with the emergence of new literary forms: in this case Middle English romance. This medieval romance is an important step in the literary apotheosis of King Richard I into the legendary Richard the Lionheart, a quintessential English hero.

Although *Richard Coeur de Lion* is characterized as a romance, that word in the Middle Ages encompassed much more than the clichéd love stories it conjures for us today, and the modern genres most analogous to medieval romance are those of the western, science fiction and fantasy.[1] In its origin in the twelfth century, the word 'romance' – *romanz* – simply signified a story told in the vernacular, or Romance, language, as opposed to Latin, the standard language of literary production in medieval Western Europe. However, over time the word, alongside such others as *estoire* (story, history) and *geste* (deed), came to describe a narrative characterized by the story of a knight's adventure, typically one of maturation, involving themes of identity and disguise, exile and return. It might involve fantastical elements, such as giants, dragons and magical amulets, but it was chiefly characterized by a new focus on interiority, and on the centrality of love between a knight and his lady.[2]

In England, in the fourteenth and fifteenth centuries, a new kind of romance emerged, typically referred to as 'Middle English popular romance' (a somewhat unwieldy title) because of its language, accessibility and audience. This is the genre to which *Richard Coeur de Lion* belongs. Before this time romance in England was composed in a dialect of French called 'Anglo-Norman' because it was the Norman Conquest of 1066 that fundamentally altered the literary landscape of England, introducing a new literary language and new literary patrons. Indeed, many Middle English romances have, or claim, a French-language source, as does *Richard Coeur de Lion* (although it is not clear whether such a source actually existed).[3] Compared to earlier French romances, *Richard Coeur de Lion* has been characterized as rough and ready, without the elevated, courtly elements that characterized twelfth-century French romance.

The narratives of Middle English popular romance tend to be lively, adventure-orientated and plot-driven, without much focus on intricate plotting or symbolic meaning. Because of this, the term 'popular' has sometimes been a way of indicating that Middle English romance was designed for and responded to the desires and concerns of a new audience. This was no longer exclusively the aristocratic, courtly audience for which earlier French-language romances were intended, but a wider audience, including bourgeois merchant and gentry families. One of the other poems of the Auchinleck Manuscript, where the earliest version of *Richard Coeur de Lion* appears, identifies its intended audience as 'children and wimmen and men/ of twelue winter elde and mare' (children and women and men of twelve years or older), suggesting that at least this compilation was designed for the ownership and use of an entire household, where English would be a shared language. The opening of *Richard Coeur de Lion* specifically identifies its intended audience as 'lewed' (l.23), or uneducated, men who do not understand French.[4] The term 'popular', therefore, has at times been intended as an implicit criticism: a suggestion that this is a genre defined by 'low aesthetic quality, unsophisticated form, and limited conceptual framework'.[5] In addition, the fact that Middle English popular romances were designed to be listened to – either read aloud or perhaps sung – as well as read silently to oneself suggests their accessibility to a wide audience. However, the word 'popular' also describes the sheer popularity of these romances; they were read, listened to, copied and enjoyed over the course of three centuries. Several, *Richard Coeur de Lion* included, made it into print in the sixteenth century, a certain indication of their continued commercial viability.

Richard Coeur de Lion, in common with much Middle English popular romance, is occupied not so much with love – although Richard does briefly have a love interest – as with crusading. The narrative keeps company with several other Middle English popular romances in the subgenre of 'crusading romance'. These romances focus on armed struggle between Christian heroes and their Muslim foes – most often termed 'Saracens' – for control of the Holy Land.[6] The general ethos of these romances is summed up trenchantly in a famous line from the twelfth-century *Song of Roland*, in which Charlemagne and his armies battle with the Muslim rulers of Spain: 'Christians are right and pagans are wrong.' These texts are not only violent but violently xenophobic. They substitute any realistic portrayal of Islam as a religion with the figure of the Saracen, the representation of which is strongly dependent on earlier twelfth- and thirteenth-century *chanson de geste*, or vernacular epic: the genre to which the *Song of Roland* belongs. The depictions of 'Saracens' in these stories are often derogatory, monstrous and what we would now think of as racialized. Take, for example, this description of

Amiete the Saracen in the twelfth-century *chanson de geste*
Fierabras:

> She was a giant blacker than pepper;
> Long in her crotch, with an enormous mouth.
> She had the height of an upright lance.
> Her eyes were redder than a lighted torch;
> She was utterly ugly and disfigured.[7]

Saracens are sometimes portrayed as noble and chivalric,
but often only to throw into relief the treasonous behaviour of
certain bad apples within the Christian contingent. In *Richard
Coeur de Lion*, for example, Richard's counterpart and antagonist
is Saladin, that is, the historical Salah al-Din Yusuf ibn Syuub
(c. 1137–1193), sultan of Egypt and Syria, and the leader of the
campaign to restore the crusader-controlled territories to Muslim
rule. In the romance the representation of Saladin as a noble and
worthy adversary coexists with absurdly fictionalized representations; one Saracen warrior is named 'Sir Gargoyle', for example
(l.4467). Along with *Richard Coeur de Lion*, which sets much of
its action on the Third Crusade, are such romances as *The Sege
of Melayne* (The Siege of Milan), in which Charlemagne must
fight alongside his nephew Roland and bishop Turpin to save the
city from attack by the Muslim sultan Arabas; and *The Sowdone
of Babylone* (The Sultan of Babylon), in which Charlemagne and
his Twelve Peers must defend Rome against the sultan Laban.
Even in romances that are not, in the first instance, about crusade, such as the popular *Bevis of Hampton* and *Guy of Warwick*,
the hero will often engage in fighting in the East, and many a
romance hero ends up an Eastern king.

As the examples above demonstrate, the 'crusade romances'
are not historical texts. Rather, they respond to the centrality
of the ideal of the Holy Land to medieval Christianity, and of

efforts to take it under (Western European) Christian control during the Middle Ages. Although the First Crusade (1096–9) was something of a surprise triumph for the crusaders, with the capture of Jerusalem and the establishment of four Crusader states in the Levant, the subsequent history of crusading is largely one of disappointment for the Christian West, with the last crusader stronghold of Acre lost in 1291, about half a century before the appearance of the earliest Middle English popular romances. By the time *Richard Coeur de Lion* was being written and adapted, the ideal of crusading remained central to Western European culture, but actual martial victories were few and far between. Importantly, the crusades were a time of cultural exchange as well as of war, and romance texts are as interested in the luxury items imported from the East, such as silks, Damascene steel and pepper, as they are in love and war. These preoccupations are evident in *Richard Coeur de Lion*. One Saracen supply caravan, for example, is described as containing

> three thousand camels,
> And there are also five hundred
> Asses and mules, and even more,
> That carry gold to Saladin,
> Refined silver, and fine treasure,
> Wheat flour and spices,
> Cloths of silk, and gold as well. (ll.6392–8)

Similarly, when Richard conquers an enemy camp, the tents are described in terms of the utmost luxury and expense:

> King Richard took the pavilions
> Of sendal and silk woven with gold.
> They were shaped like castles,
> With pennons of gold and silver.

Many noble tales were
Written thereon of wild beasts –
Tigers, dragons, lions, leopards –
And all this King Richard won.
Bound coffers and great sacks
He had there, without number.
They had won so much treasure
That they didn't know where to put it all. (ll.5155–67)

So, crusade romances might best be understood as examples of fantasy wish-fulfilment, and this is an important context for *Richard Coeur de Lion*, which in its representation of Richard's crusade offers a tangled web of revisionist history and flat-out wishful thinking.

Fewer than a hundred Middle English romances have survived, and *Richard Coeur de Lion* seems to have been one of the most popular, judging from the number of copies that have come down to us. These are seven manuscripts (some incomplete) and two printed editions by the London publisher Wynkyn de Worde dated 1509 and 1528. Admittedly, this is not a huge quantity compared to the number of extant manuscripts of Chaucer's *The Canterbury Tales* (about 92, some fragmentary) or the most popular of all Middle English poems, *The Pricke of Conscience* (more than 120). This relatively large number of surviving manuscripts, however, poses its own complications. No two of these manuscripts are identical, and they differ more dramatically even than one might expect from a culture in which literature had to be copied by hand. Entire episodes are included in some manuscripts but not in others, and in some cases an episode is presented very differently between manuscripts. One scholar has suggested that 'at least ten authors had a hand in the composition' of the Richard the Lionheart family of romances.[8] Moreover, none of the surviving manuscripts seems to have been the direct

Title page of *Kynge Rycharde cuer du lyon* (London, 1528 edn published by Wynkyn de Worde).

source for any other. Indeed, the romance even goes by different titles in the manuscripts: *Kyng Richard* in its earliest version, but also *The Romance of King Richard the Conqueror* and *The Life of King Richard I*.[9]

Because all the manuscripts of *Richard Coeur de Lion* are different, most are incomplete or fragmentary and none contains what might be called a 'definitive' version of the romance. In many ways it may be more accurate to think of a '*Richard Coeur de Lion* tradition': that is to say, a series of episodes in romance form about the exploits of a famous king now passing into legend.[10] Almost all medieval romance is episodic in nature, and many medieval romances exist in slightly different versions.[11] The familiar stories of King Arthur and his Knights of the Round Table are a good example of this, in that there are always more adventures to have, more quests to undertake. In *Richard Coeur de Lion*, sometimes a self-contained episode will identify itself as such. After Richard's successful capture of Acre, for example, the romance marks a transition in topic by pausing to introduce the spring motif, most famous from Chaucer's *Canterbury Tales* (which begins 'Whan that Aprill with his shoures soote/ The droghte of March hath perced to the roote'):

> Whoever wants to learn more about his brave deeds,
> Listen now, and you may hear.
> It's delightful in the month of May
> When birds sing their songs;
> Flowers bloom on apple and pear trees,
> Small birds sing merrily, and
> Ladies strew their bowers
> With red roses and lily flowers. (ll.3757–64)

After this episode the beginning of a new episode is again signalled with the spring motif: 'Before Saint James's Day,/ When birds begin to chirp merrily,/ King Richard turned his host to pass/ Toward the city of Haifa' (ll.4817–18). Romance episodes tend to be self-contained narrative units that do not substantially affect the course or development of other episodes. In *Richard Coeur de Lion*, for instance, one episode tells of his demon mother, another tells of his imprisonment in Germany, and yet another tells of his capture of Acre. None of these has any influence on the action of any other, and each individual episode tends not to be recalled or referred to in the text. (This sometimes results in significant loose ends, however, such as the magic rings given to Richard by the king of Germany which are never referred to again.)

The content of *Richard Coeur de Lion*'s episodes exists on a continuum between history and fiction. Some of these episodes stick pretty closely to the historical record, as do those that describe Richard's successful siege of Acre. Others depart completely from the historical record, as in the episode that claims his mother was an Eastern princess named Cassodorien rather than the historical Eleanor of Aquitaine. This episodic structure creates a sense of seriality that lends itself to expansion, subtraction and substitution. Some episodes of the *Richard Coeur de Lion* romance, in particular Richard's adventures in Messina, Cyprus and Acre, appear in all the manuscripts, and they seem to have constituted the core of what the romance tradition felt was important about Richard the Lionheart.[12] They may be an attempt to view what was ultimately the failure of the Third Crusade through the rose-tinted glasses of romance. Indeed, Richard's crusading successes, especially the siege and capture of Acre, constitute a shared story element of all the extant versions of *Richard Coeur de Lion*, and are at the core of the romance's vision of Richard as a crusading king. Other episodes, such as the story of Richard's demon mother, appear in relatively few of the surviving manuscripts. Together, these romance versions of Richard's life represent a

Medieval fortress of Acre, the scene of Richard's great success in the romance.

flexible tradition of mythmaking surrounding the famous king. Overall, the romance that we now call *Richard Coeur de Lion* is probably better thought of as a series of related romances about Richard I, each selective of which aspects of the emerging legend of Richard it wishes to tell, and each free to introduce new elements to the legend, borrowed either from the world of romance or from the legendary stories that already surrounded Richard, or from both.

Several of the *Richard Coeur de Lion* manuscripts, including the Auchinleck's *King Richard*, open with a preface situating Richard among the great heroes of antiquity and of romance:

Lord Jesus, King of Glory,
What grace and victory
You sent to King Richard,
Who was never found to be a coward!

It is very good to hear tales
Of his prowess and his conquests.
Men make many new romances
Of good knights, strong and true;
Both in England and in France
Men read of their deeds in romances:
Or Roland and of Oliver,
And all of Charlemagne's twelve peers,
Of Alexander and of Charlemagne,
Of King Arthur and of Gawain,
How they were good and courteous knights;
Men read in rhyme of Turpin,
And of Ogier Daneys, and of Troy,
About the war there in olden times:
Of Hector, and of Achilles,
And of the folk they slew in that combat.
But these poems are written in French books:
Uneducated men don't understand them,
For uneducated men don't know French –
Barely one among a hundred.
And nevertheless, with good cheer,
I understand that many of them
Would like to hear of the noble deeds
Of the valiant knights of England. (ll.1–28)

This preface proudly inscribes Richard in the company of the legendary heroes of the romance tradition. It includes figures from antiquity (Achilles, Hector, Alexander), from the legendary history of Charlemagne (Roland, Oliver, Turpin, Ogier the Dane) and from pure legend (Arthur, Gawain).[13] Together, all these heroes embody the ethos of medieval chivalry, where knights are strong, and true, and good, and courteous. The list emphasizes kingship, itemizing great knights and heroes who are also kings, such as Alexander, Charlemagne and Arthur. In this regard, it perhaps inadvertently highlights Richard's anomalousness in this company; it is extremely unusual for a more or less contemporary figure to become the hero of a romance, which mostly cloaks its action in a nostalgia-drenched past.[14] *Richard Coeur de Lion* repeats this formula towards the end of the romance, prefacing Richard's siege of Jaffa (ll.6711–22). Here the list may be used to signal the beginning of a self-contained episode, as with the invocations of spring in the lines 'It's delightful in the month of May/ When birds sing their songs'. In this second list the poet repeats the figures of Alexander the Great, Charlemagne, Achilles, Arthur and Gawain, but adds in addition to other classical and French heroes the English Bevis of Hampton and Guy of Warwick. The prefatory verses stake a claim for the Englishness of *Richard Coeur de Lion* in contrast to a tradition it identifies as French; because romances tend to be written in French, the preface claims, uneducated men cannot understand them. Nevertheless, these men, implicitly *English* men, want to hear about the deeds of English heroes. This explicit juxtaposition of English versus French is a theme not only of the preface but of the poem, as we shall see.

The first of *Richard Coeur de Lion*'s rather dramatic romance episodes is the story of Cassodorien, Richard's fairy (or demon) mother. The earliest version of the romance, *King Richard*, makes no mention of Richard's family, but rather gets right down to the action of crusading. By the fifteenth century, however, a fictional version of Richard's family history had been added to the tradition, a version that had roots in Richard's own lifetime. The story begins with Richard's father, King Henry, and his search for a wife. Henry sends out messengers to scour the lands for a wife wealthy and beautiful enough for him. Becalmed on the sea, the messengers come across a magnificent white ship with a lady 'bright as the sun through a glass' (l.76). Her father is King Corbaryng of Antioch, and he has had a vision that he and his daughter Cassodorien should go to England. They do, and she is introduced to King Henry amid great pageantry:

> The damsel was led on to land,
> And cloths of gold spread before her,
> And her father together with her.
> With an excellent crown of gold,
> And the messengers on every side,
> And minstrels with great pride. (ll.143–8)

Henry and Cassodorien are subsequently married. The great surprise here, of course, is that, in reality, Henry II's wife was not the Eastern princess Cassodorien, but rather the French Eleanor of Aquitaine. Some of the versions of *Richard Coeur de Lion* hew closer to history and acknowledge Eleanor as Richard's mother, rather than the fictional Cassodorien. The equally fictional King Corbaryng of Antioch is an interesting addition, however, because he appears elsewhere in the annals of crusading romance. He is the defeated defender of Antioch in *La Chanson d'Antioche* (The Song of Antioch), a twelfth- or early thirteenth-century *chanson de geste* about the First Crusade. *La Chanson d'Antioche* is part of a cycle of crusade romances that centres on the historical figure of Godfrey of Bouillon, a hero of the First Crusade and the first king of the Latin Kingdom of Jerusalem. The romance cycle begins by connecting Godfrey with the legend of the Swan Knight. In this story, the seven children of a king and queen are transformed into swans, although they are subsequently able to return to human form. One of these, known as the Swan Knight, becomes the grandfather of Godfrey of Bouillon. The romance then turns to a more historical account of the capture of Antioch during the First Crusade, which sees Godfrey and his fellow crusaders defeat 'King Corbaran' and capture Antioch.[15] This cycle of romances, including *La Chanson d'Antioche*, was immensely popular throughout the Middle Ages, and its fame elevated Godfrey to the ranks of the 'Nine Worthies'. *Richard Coeur de Lion* surely borrows the figure of King Corbaryng from this tradition. In so doing, the romance purposefully seeks to affiliate itself to this group of texts now known as the Old French crusade cycle.[16]

To this end, the romance provides a supernatural origin story for Richard, analogous to Godfrey's descent from the Swan Knight. The marriage of Henry and Cassodorien is, initially, happy, and they have two sons, Richard and John, and a daughter, Topaz. But Cassodorien has an eccentricity: at her wedding Mass, she faints at the sight of the elevation of the consecrated eucharist, and she subsequently refuses to witness it again. This situation persists for fifteen years until, on the advice of one of his barons, Henry forces her to stay to the end of the service. This plan backfires, as Cassodorien grabs John and Topaz by the hands and flies out through the roof.[17] She accidentally drops John, but she holds on to Topaz, and neither of them is seen again.

This strange story has its source in the Angevin dynasty's own origin myth. The twelfth-century writer Gerald of Wales tells a very similar tale of the wife of Fulk Nerra (a legendary ancestor of Richard), who similarly, when forced to witness the Mass, grabs her children and flies out of the church through a window. Gerald recounts Richard I himself referencing this story, and commenting of his family that 'they had all come of the devil, and to the devil they would go.'[18] This strange episode appears to be designed to lend credence to the number of times his enemies will characterize Richard as 'a devil and no man'. With the story of the marriage of Henry and Cassodorien, *Richard Coeur de Lion* announces its generic affiliations and stakes its claim for Richard's reinvention as a hero of romance. Like Godfrey, Richard is a crusading hero now passing into legend.

Another story element that *Richard Coeur de Lion* shares with other contemporary romances is the motif of the 'Three Day Tournament'. In this motif, which is common to several medieval romances, a knight will fight under the cloak of anonymity, wearing a different disguise on each day of the tournament and demonstrating remarkable prowess. At the end of these tournaments the anonymous knight is unmasked and crowned the winner. In the longest version of *Richard Coeur de Lion*, no sooner has his mother abandoned him than we find Richard crowned king and hosting a tournament where he himself plays the role of the anonymous knight. In a variation on the Three Day Tournament, Richard fights in three disguises in a single day: first in black, then in red, then white. In black he vanquishes his first opponents easily. He has somewhat less luck in red and white, since his subsequent opponents fight back hardily. In the end, however, these two opponents turn out to be two of Richard's barons – Fulk D'Oilly and Thomas Multoun – and the tournament has been a test of sorts, because Richard intends these knights to accompany him on a secret reconnaissance mission to the Holy Land. At the end of the episode they head off together, disguised as pilgrims. Subsequent to this adventure, discussed later, Fulk and Thomas accompany Richard on crusade, where Fulk will lead a siege of the city of Ebedy (ll.4304–625) and Thomas a siege of Castle Orgellous (ll.3973–4302). The latter castle borrows its name from an earlier romance about Percival, one of King Arthur's knights. As this detail suggests, these adventures are entirely fictional; Richard never hosted a tournament, nor did he ever travel in disguise to Jerusalem. However, the naming of his companions may provide a clue to the origins of the romance. Fulk D'Oilly and Thomas Multoun were not twelfth-century contemporaries of Richard I, but rather names that refer to prominent baronial families with histories of crusading ancestors. Their inclusion may indicate that these families, related by marriage, were the patrons of one version of this romance.

If these episodes introducing Richard's supernatural mother and his disguised participation in a tournament clearly draw inspiration from other romances in reimagining Richard as a romance hero, the following episode demonstrates most clearly the power of romance to rewrite history. In 1192, on his return from crusade, Richard I was captured and imprisoned by Leopold V, duke of Austria, delivered to Henry VI, the Holy Roman Emperor, and held for ransom. The cost was enormous: at over 150,000 marks, it represented more than twice Richard's annual income from his English lands.[19] *Richard Coeur de Lion* reimagines this historical disaster, with a canny rewriting of imprisonment as heroics. For the romance introduces a fundamental change to the timeline of the historical events by having Richard, along with his trusty companions Fulk and Thomas, captured in 'Almayne' (Germany) before, rather than after, his crusade.

In the romance's version, Richard has returned from his scouting mission to the Holy Land and is passing through Germany on his way home when he is betrayed by a minstrel to whom he has failed to offer hospitality. This version of Germany, however, is a fanciful one, ruled by King Modred (whose name recalls King Arthur's nephew and antagonist Mordred). Rather than suffer an ignominious imprisonment, Richard rescues himself and earns his famous sobriquet 'lionheart'. First, he is visited in his imprisonment by the German king's son Wardrew, who offers him a competition: this is the folklore motif of the exchange of blows, or 'pluck buffet'. Richard accepts, and Wardrew 'gave Richard a clout on the ear/ so that fire sprang out of his eyes' (ll.760–61). The next day, when it is Richard's turn to deliver a blow, he cheats by wrapping his hand in a mixture of straw and wax, effectively turning it into a deadly weapon. Sure enough, the blow he delivers kills Wardrew. The German king and queen are overcome with grief at the loss of their son, and the king, determining that Richard must die for this act, throws him in prison.

Fortunately, Richard is rescued from this predicament by the king's daughter Margery, who instantly falls in love with him, and has him provided with food and clothing and, scandalously, brought to her room at night. When this is discovered, the king is predictably enraged, but prevented by honour and the law from killing a fellow king outright. It is therefore decided to send a starving lion into Richard's cell to kill him. However, warned and aided by Margery, Richard instead kills the lion, ripping its heart from its chest. He then brings the bloody heart into the king's hall and eats it in front of the assembled court:

> He took the heart still warm,
> And brought it into the hall,
> Before the king and all his men.
> The king sat at dinner on the dais,
> With dukes and earls, proud in the company.
> The salt cellar stood on the table.
> Richard pressed out all the blood,
> And wet the heart in the salt –
> The King and all his men looked on –
> Without bread he ate the heart. (ll. 1100–109)

At this point the German king exclaims that Richard should indeed be known as the Lionheart.[20]

The whole episode is a bizarre interweaving of the legends that were circulating about Richard's captivity, the motif of the exchange of blows (shared with other romances, such as the better-known *Sir Gawain and the Green Knight*), and romantic love. It offers the most typical romance motif of a love interest for Richard in the form of Margery, daughter of the king of Germany. Love relationships are important to the psychology

of romance because they offer a glimpse of interiority, of characters' thoughts and feelings that might otherwise be lost in the
headlong rush to adventure. This psychological aspect of romance,
however, is largely absent from Richard and Margery's relationship. We are introduced to Margery and told that she loves
Richard within the space of four lines, without any explanation
as to why:

> The King's daughter was in her chamber,
> With her maidens of honour:
> Margery was her name.
> She loved Richard with all her heart. (ll.881–4)

Richard's emotions are similarly obscure. When he is brought to
Margery's chamber, we are simply told that he 'amused himself
with her as he wished' (l.920). In this regard, the representation
of Margery in *Richard Coeur de Lion* lays bare what scholars
describe as the 'homosociality' of medieval romance. This is to
say that, although we often find strong female characters, such
as Margery, who seem to act on their own desires and are rarely
censured for doing so, their chief narrative purpose tends to be
to regulate and negotiate relationships between men. This might
be in their role as heiresses, who transfer land from their fathers
to their husbands through marriage, or as intercessors, whose
wielding of the soft power of affect can be a means of avoiding
violence – and this is the case with Margery.

The episode reframes the unfortunate story of Richard's captivity as one of active heroism, and he emerges from the episode
as Richard 'the Lionheart'. His bravery and heroism are emphasized, and when the German king demands half of England's
wealth to free him, it seems a fair exchange, since Richard has
killed his son and his lion and seduced his daughter. Indeed,
the grief of the king at all the wrongs Richard has done him is

emphasized. This episode is an important element of the *Richard Coeur de Lion* romance tradition, and is present in almost all the manuscripts. The need to reclaim what was clearly a traumatic episode in England's history seems to have played a large part in the composition of this romance. When Richard makes a point of returning to Germany on his way to crusade, in order to reclaim his expensive ransom, Modred seems anxious and tries to starve Richard's armies by refusing to let them buy food. However, Richard receives a warm welcome from Margery, who once again proves extremely helpful. She reconciles him with her father, who returns Richard's treasure quite happily:

> King Modred said, 'My gracious son,
> I will swear upon a book,
> That which I took from you is ready
> If you will have it, and much more
> I shall give you, to make my peace'.
> King Richard took him in his arms,
> And kissed him very many times:
> They were friends and made merriment.
> (ll.1606–14)

In addition, Modred gives Richard two magic rings: one that protects its wearer from drowning and another that protects from fire. Once this episode has ended, however, these rings – along with Margery – are completely forgotten, as we have seen, and never reappear in the story.[21] Overall, the romance shows significant interest in rewriting the history of Richard's German captivity, and the point of this episode is to redeem him in this regard. By recasting a historical disaster as a triumph, the episode of Richard the Lionheart's German captivity offers a great example of romance's wishful thinking and of the cultural work that romance is primed to do.

Released from his German captivity, Richard returns home to London, calls a session of Parliament and proposes a crusade to recapture Jerusalem, which was lost to the armies of Saladin. After his successful detour through Germany he proceeds to Messina, Sicily, where he meets King Philip of France. No sooner has Richard arrived in Sicily than 'the King of France thought of a treason/ Against King Richard without delay' (1677–8). Philip sends King Tancred of Sicily a poison-pen letter alleging that Richard is plotting to overthrow him. While at first Tancred is enraged, cooler heads prevail, and Tancred and Richard are reconciled. The letter, however, serves to portray the king of France as inherently treacherous. During their time together in Sicily the French and the Greeks (derogatively called 'Gryphons') gang up on the English and attack them with impunity:

> The English men went into the market,
> And often took hard blows:
> The French and the Gryphons openly
> Slew our English knights there. (ll.1769–72)

As a result the first battle of the romance is not between Christians and Saracens, as might be expected of a crusade romance, but instead between the English and the French, as the romancer emphasizes 'our English knights' (l.1772). The English win handily and loot the city where the French have been staying:

> They broke open coffers and took treasure:
> Gold and silver and cloths,
> Jewels, stones, and spices,
> And all that they found in treasuries.
> There was no one of English blood
> Who didn't have as much gold
> As he could carry. (ll.1949–55)[22]

The episode ends with the king of France abasing himself before King Richard and begging for reconciliation.

This must have been a very satisfying scenario for a medieval English audience of *Richard Coeur de Lion* in view of the context of the Hundred Years War. Without a doubt there was significant mistrust between Philip and Richard during the Third Crusade itself. Philip left the Holy Land and, in the language of the English chroniclers, 'abandoned' his crusade after the crusaders' success at Acre. He proceeded to return to France and collude with Richard's brother John to undermine Richard's French possessions and, indeed, his rule in England. Nevertheless, at the time of the composition and adaptation of the *Richard Coeur de Lion* family of romances, England faced a new competition with France, one that had its roots in the twelfth-century disputes over England's French territories, and which both created and fed off an incipient sense of nationalism in both countries. The Hundred Years War (so called because it lasted, with interim truces, from 1337 to 1453) had its proximate cause in the death of Charles IV of France in 1328 without a male heir. At that time King Edward III of England was Charles's nephew, the son of his sister Isabella, and thus his closest male descendant. The French nobility, however – perhaps unhappy at the thought of an English king – denied that the crown could be inherited through the female line, and instead selected Philip, count of Valois (a cousin of Charles on his father's side), to be king. Edward ultimately went to war in order to assert his right to the French crown. As in all wars, propaganda played its part, and anti-French rhetoric became increasingly common in English writings during this period.[23] The ongoing Hundred Years War with France is one important context of reception for the romance, and it is very likely to have influenced the representation of the struggles of a heroic English king against a faithless French king, even as this representation would seem to undermine their shared cause in the crusade.

A long, self-contained episode in the second half of the romance (ll.3759–4816), in which Richard and Philip engage in some wholly fictional battles and sieges after the fall of Acre, seems designed solely to highlight differences between the two rulers, between the English and the French, in ways that are un-flattering to the latter. The episode dwells more on the unenviable characteristics of the French than on those of the Saracens, whom they are both purportedly fighting:

> French men are timid and faint,
> And Saracens are cunning and crafty,
> And ingenious in their deeds.
> The French men are covetous.
> When they sit at the tavern,
> There they are brave and bold
> To speak boastful words,
> And brag about their deeds.
> They're of little worth and foolishly proud:
> They can only fight with loud words,
> And say that no man is their peer –
> But when they come to a dangerous situation,
> And see men begin to deal strokes,
> Then they quickly turn tail,
> And begin to draw in their horns
> Like a snail among the thorns. (ll.3849–64)

The episode begins with Richard inviting Philip to a feast (l.3773ff), at which he distributes gifts to his followers. He advises Philip to do the same, but Philip declines, and Richard's gener-osity is explicitly contrasted to Philip's stinginess. Even worse, when Richard advises Philip to kill all the inhabitants of the towns he captures, rather than ransom them, Philip again declines to do so. In the end Richard captures the towns that Philip had

allowed to ransom themselves, then speaks to him in conde-
scending language: 'Certainly, Philip, you are not wise./ You're
forgiven the first transgression;/ You may learn from this, if you
will' (ll.4784–6). In the end, it is implied that even Richard's
failure to capture Jerusalem is Philip's fault. One day, seemingly
out of the blue, Philip turns to Richard and insists that Jerusalem
should be his: 'King Richard, listen to me!/ That rich City of
Jerusalem/ Even though you win it, it shall be mine!' (ll.5895–7).
Richard is understandably enraged, and refuses to help Philip with
the conquest. In turn, Philip becomes 'sick with ire' (l.5911) and
decides to go home to France.²⁴ This reframing of Philip's decision to leave the crusade from a canny political one driven by
events back home into a fit of pique is characteristic of the treatment of Richard's crusading partner in *Richard Coeur de Lion*.
The antagonism that existed between the two men on crusade
and the deterioration of the relationship between them are captured, but also extended from a personal competition for land
and power to delineate purported nationalistic characteristics
for the French and the English.

From Sicily Richard attempts to sail to Acre to begin his crusade, but once again fate intervenes. A storm shipwrecks his fleet
in Cyprus, where the locals kill the English and steal their treasure. There follows an exciting episode that fictionalizes Richard's
overthrow of the emperor of Cyprus, Isaac Comnenus, and
retrieval (once again) of his treasure. The episode shows, for the
first time, Richard wielding his battle-axe, a rather unchivalric
weapon in the romance tradition, but one that stands Richard
in good stead. The poet writes:

> King Richard, I understand,
> Before he went out of England,
> Had an axe made for the occasion,
> In order to break the Saracens' bones. (ll.2209–12)

The episode repeats the theme that you anger King Richard – 'who was never found a coward' (l.2008), the poem repeats – at your peril.

When Richard finally arrives at Acre, his first battle is at sea, when a ship full of Saracens attempting to supply a blockaded Acre pretend to be French. Richard sees through their ruse, and a battle is undertaken:

> Arrows and bolts flew between them
> As thickly, without cease,
> As hail after a thunderclap.
> And in the battle that was so fierce,
> King Richard came into the Saracen ship.
> When he had come on in haste, he placed his back against
>   the mast.
> Whoever he reached with his axe,
> He hastily received his death.
> Some he hit on the helmet
> So that he cleaved them to the chin,
> And some to the waist,
> And some to the ship's deck.
> Some he struck in the neck
> So that head and helmet flew into the sea.
> For no armour withstood his axe,
> No more than wax withstands a knife. (ll.2562–78)

The battle is won, and Richard breaks the chain that bars Acre's harbour with his axe – thus making a spectacular entrance to his crusade. This episode, interestingly enough, is largely historical, and an example of the ways in which the truth of Richard the Lionheart's life is sometimes stranger than fiction.[25]

This description of the battle on board the Saracen ship is characteristic of the portrayal of war in *Richard Coeur de Lion*.

Richard bearing his signature battle-axe, miniature from the Auchinleck Manuscript, 1330s.

One-on-one encounters between mounted knights are high-lighted, and individual valour emphasized. Bodies and horses are cleaved in two, heads roll around the ground, arrows fly thick as rain. There is a delight in the dramatic strategies of war, such as scaling castle walls, Greek fire and, above all, siege engines. Richard has some spectacular siege engines. One, called 'Robynet', hurls stones at the walls of Acre (l.2922). Another, 'Mate-Gryphon' (Greek-killer), is six storeys high; at the siege of Acre Richard fits it with a mangonel, or catapult, which hurls bee-hives into the city (l.2909). The deck of his ship features a windmill that is lit from within by torches so that it glows, and instead of grinding grain it appears to gush blood on to some sort of statue covered in blood, which the Saracens take for a devil (ll.2650–80). In these battle scenes historical figures are

fictionalized and mingle with purely fictional characters. The
overall design seems to be to rewrite crusade history, countering
Saladin's important victories at Hattin and Jerusalem with
descriptions of Richard's triumph at the (historical) battle of
Arsuf and the (fictional) battle of Babylon.[26]

Upon Richard's arrival at Acre the crusaders there describe
the suffering they have gone through in the past seven years: a
catalogue of disasters, including a famine so serious that they are
forced to eat their horses. Hearing this, Richard leaps into action
and, through a combination of strength and ingenuity (those
beehives!), brings down the outer wall of the city of Acre, enabling the crusaders to occupy it. The Saracens within signal for
help and Saladin arrives with a huge army; now the situation is
reversed, and the besiegers are the besieged. It is in this context
that perhaps the strangest series of episodes in the romance occur.
Richard has not been on crusade for long, but the foreign climate
does not suit him and he falls ill. He loses his appetite and longs

Trebuchet seen in a miniature from the Crusader Bible depicting
the Old Testament story of Saul and his army defeating Nahash
and the Ammonites, *c.* 1244–54.

for the flavour of pork. His men cannot find a pig to slaughter, so, fearing for the king's health (and also fearing his wrath), they substitute the next best thing: a Saracen. An old knight advises:

> Take a Saracen young and fat.
> In haste let the scoundrel be slain,
> Cut open, and skinned,
> And boiled very quickly
> With seasoning, and spices,
> And with saffron of good colour.
> When the King smells the scent thereof,
> As long as his fever has broken,
> He will have a good appetite for it.
> When he has had a good taste,
> And eaten a good meal,
> And drunk a mouthful of the broth,
> Slept afterwards, and sweated a drop,
> Through God's might, and my counsel,
> Soon he will be refreshed and healthy. (ll.3088–102)

The strange scheme works! The king eats and sleeps, and when he wakes he feels recovered enough to go back into battle. After his exertions, Richard fears a relapse and asks for more of the delicious pork dinner he enjoyed the night before; specifically, he asks for the pig's head. When the cook demurs that he no longer has the head, Richard demands to see it. The suspense of the moment builds and the cook fears the worst, but, at a loss for what else to do, he produces the head of the Saracen on a platter. Richard's response is unexpected:

> When the King saw his dark face,
> His black beard, and his white teeth,
> And how his lips grinned wide,

The King cried, 'What devil is this!'
And began to laugh as if he were mad.
'What, is Saracens' flesh this good,
And I never knew it until now?
By God's death and his resurrection,
We shall never die for hunger
While we may, in any assault,
Slay Saracens, take their flesh,
Boil them and roast them and bake them,
And gnaw their flesh to the bones.
Now that I have proved it once,
Before hunger makes me wretched,
I and my folk shall eat more!' (ll.3211–26)

As strange and absurd as this episode seems, a historical event may lie behind it. Three different eyewitness accounts of the First Crusade describe crusaders, driven by starvation in the desert, resorting to cannibalizing the bodies of the dead. Raymond d'Aguilers, in his *Historia francorum qui ceperunt Iherusalem* (History of the Franks Who Captured Jerusalem), describes the situation in the following manner:

Now the food shortage became so acute that the
Christians ate with gusto many rotten Saracen bodies
which they had pitched into the swamps two or three
weeks before. This spectacle disgusted as many crusaders as
it did strangers, and as a result of it many gave up without
hope of Frankish reinforcements and turned back. The
Saracens and Turks reacted thus: 'This stubborn and
merciless race, unmoved by hunger, sword or other perils
for one year at Antioch, now feasts on human flesh;
therefore, we ask, 'who can resist them?' The infidels
spread stories of those and other inhuman acts of the

crusaders, but we were unaware that God had made us an object of terror.[27]

Whether or not this story of crusader cannibalism was percolating in the popular imagination, cannibalism as a metaphor is extremely resonant. It encompasses the paradox that in order to be a cannibal one must be human, but the very act of cannibalism is inhuman. Richard's laughter in response to his unwitting cannibalism defuses the horror of the situation, but it also establishes his persona as somewhat monstrous. If his consumption of the lion's heart made him Richard the Lionheart, the romance seems implicitly to ask, what does his consumption of Saracen flesh make him?

Moreover, Richard is quick to pick up on the strategic aspects of crusader cannibalism hinted at by Raymond. Shortly after this episode, a Saracen messenger arrives with an offer to surrender the city (l.3245). At first, he offers to surrender both Acre and Jerusalem, with the proviso that the 'marquis of Montferrat' be crowned king of Syria. Richard protests loudly, insisting that the marquis is a traitor who has abandoned Christianity and become a Saracen. King Philip of France is more circumspect, and defends the marquis, although Richard's wrath takes the day. It also shows a new breach opening between Richard and Philip, and the suggestion that Richard is more appropriately warlike, whereas Philip's allegiances are questionable.

With the rejection of this first offer, the messenger offers instead to surrender Acre alone, along with the Holy Cross, and to offer hostages as proof of Saladin's good faith. This offer is accepted, and Richard takes control of Acre. When the Saracens arrive with money and treasure to redeem their hostages, however, their reception is not quite what they expect; they are greeted with a gruesome cannibal banquet. Inviting the Saracen envoys to dinner, Richard has served as a first course the boiled heads of his Saracen prisoners, each with his name inscribed on his forehead. As the envoys recoil in horror and grief at being served the heads of their friends and family members for dinner, Richard sits at the head of the table and feasts gleefully on the head that has been served to him. When he sees that his guests are not eating, he has the heads replaced with a more appropriate feast, but it is too late; the envoys are not hungry, and Richard has made his point. He finishes the banquet with a threat: his men will never go hungry on their crusade while they can simply eat the enemy:

> 'None of us shall die for hunger
> While we may go into battle
> And slay the Saracens outright,
> Wash the flesh, and roast the head.
> With one Saracen I may well feed
> Fully nine, or ten,
> Of my good Christian men.'
> King Richard said, 'I guarantee you,
> There is no flesh so nourishing
> For an English Christian man –
> Nor partridge nor plover, heron nor swan,
> Cow nor ox, sheep nor swine,
> As is the flesh of Saracen! (ll.3540–52)

When the envoys return home and recount this terrible ordeal to Saladin, one of them describes Richard violently gnawing 'the flesh with his teeth,/ Acting like a mad lion' (ll.3609–10). Cannibalism here becomes a metaphor for conquest, as Richard threatens literally to incorporate his enemies. The scene also transforms religious difference into national difference: Saracen flesh is nourishing to *English* Christian men. Although profoundly disturbing, the romance casts Richard's barbarism here as a positive aspect of English identity, and it never questions it from a moral or ethical point of view.

The envoys are truly horrified by what they have witnessed, and they beg Saladin to do everything in his power to appease Richard and end the war before Richard has a chance to make good on his threat. Taking their advice, Saladin sends messengers to Richard, promising to make him king of Syria, Egypt and more, if only he will 'forsake Jesus/ and take Muhammed as his lord' (ll.3703–4). Predictably, Richard angrily refuses and demands instead the return of the Holy Cross, which was captured by Saladin along with Jerusalem. When the messengers claim they do not know where it is, Richard takes his revenge by ordering his men to kill all the Saracen hostages – an act that is sanctioned by God through an angel who cries (in French), 'Lords, kill! Kill!' (l.3749). It is difficult not to see some degree of discomfort with Richard's historical massacre of his hostages lying behind these two stories. This is even more the case in the following episode, where King Philip's reluctance to kill his prisoners, choosing instead to let them ransom themselves, is part of a series of contrasts that are drawn between the two kings, as we have seen: contrasts that are intended to be unflattering to Philip.

The final thousand or so lines of the romance return, more or less, to the historical trajectory of Richard's crusade, as it is described in such chronicles as Ambroise's *Estoire de la Guerre Sainte* (History of the Holy War), which may be the 'French' source that the romance alludes to (l.5098). It references the historical battles of Jaffa and Ascalon alongside some fictional ones, such as Richard's battles for 'Nineveh' and 'Babylon'. Throughout it transmutes history into epic, placing a strong emphasis on action. The narrative moves forwards quickly and consists almost entirely of depictions of battle, especially single combat. It is peppered with the names of crusader heroes, such as James of Avesnes, Garnier de Nablus and William Longespée: names that are no longer so well known as that of Richard the Lionheart.[28] In these scenes Richard's leadership and bravery are everywhere evidenced. As the romancer says, 'his deeds were praiseworthy, as was his fame' (l.5172).

Here, as elsewhere, the romancer cannot resist the fantastical for too long, as demonstrated by the episode in which Saladin attempts to trick Richard by offering him a magic horse. This episode reimagines an event recorded by several chroniclers, in which Saladin offered to make Richard the gift of a horse.[29] Ambroise, for example, describes Saladin's brother arriving:

> he came galloping up with two Arab horses which
> he sent to the king of England, beseeching him and
> begging him, because of his valiant deeds, which he,
> Saphadin, knew and because of his boldness, that he
> would mount one [of the horses] on condition that, if
> God brought them out of this safe and sound that if he
> lived then Richard would ensure that he received some
> reward. He later received a large recompense. The king
> took them willingly and said that he would take many
> such, if they came from his most mortal enemy, as was
> his need.[30]

In the romance Saladin offers Richard both a horse and single combat. Cunningly, he gets a necromancer to conjure two demon horses. One, a colt, will kneel to suckle at the sound of its mother's neigh – thereby exposing Richard's neck to Saladin's sword in their combat. Luckily, an angel alerts Richard to this nefarious plan, and Richard stops up the colt's ears with wax, thus neutralizing the threat. The angel further advises Richard to tie a tree trunk across the horse's saddle, with which it will wreak destruction on everything in its path. In this way Richard wins the day (although unfortunately, and rather humorously, the tree tied to his saddle prevents him from following a fleeing Saladin into the forest; ll.5530ff).

This story, or a similar one, was popular in the visual arts, as well as possibly having been transmitted orally. In the middle of the thirteenth century King Henry III had the scene of single combat between Richard the Lionheart and Saladin painted on the walls of one of his palaces. Although the painting has not survived, a rendering of the combat does survive on the Chertsey Tiles (c. 1250). Henry III and his wife, Eleanor of Provence, probably commissioned these tiles for the Palace of Westminster; they were discovered at Chertsey Abbey in the nineteenth century.[31] In the next century the scene perhaps again appears in the margins of the Luttrell Psalter, although this iconography might also represent the triumph of a crusader over his Muslim foe more generally. The popularity of the scene may be the reason the romancer included it here, as further evidence of Richard's personal prowess as a crusader.[32]

As the battle scenes continue, Richard receives bad news from home: his brother John is planning to usurp the kingdom

Floor tiles depicting Richard and Saladin battle, Chertsey Abbey, England, c. 1250–60, earthenware.

Richard and Saladin battle at Jaffa, marginalia from the Luttrell Psalter, 1325–35.

and to have himself crowned on Easter Day (ll.6322ff). Richard is angered and concerned, but reluctant to leave until he kills Saladin and regains the Holy Land. He wonders if he should go home to reclaim his kingdom, then return to finish his business in the Holy Land. In the event, an angel makes the decision for him, advising him to

> Make a truce, and let your barons
> Go to the river and do their pilgrimage
> To Nazareth and to Bethlehem,
> To Calvary and to Jerusalem,
> And then let them travel homeward,
> And you follow after with your shipmen,
> For you have enemies, I understand,
> Both here and in your own land. (ll.6953–60)

So the romance ends, not with Richard's victory on crusade, but with his death in Europe. The romancer conflates the stories of Richard's imprisonment by Leopold of Austria upon his return from crusade and that of his death by a stray arrow at the siege of Châlus-Chabrol. The plot of *Richard Coeur de Lion* jumps from the Holy Land to Castle Gaillard in France. The day is hot, and when Richard takes off his helmet to cool down, one of the duke of Austria's spies treacherously shoots him in the head with an arrow. Richard and his men take the castle, but he dies of the wound. The romance ends with him buried next to his father at Fontevraud:

> King Richard was a conqueror.
> God give his soul much honour!
> No more is said of him in English,
> But may Jesus who dearly bought us
> Grant his soul peace and rest,
> And ours, too, when it comes there,
> And that it may be so,
> All say amen, for charity. (ll.7233–40)

Richard Coeur de Lion is a national and nationalizing romance, constructing an English identity over and against its enemies, here imagined as both French and Muslim. Richard the Lionheart, the romance insists, leads men 'of Englysshe blode' (l.1953). The romance defines an English sense of self over and against its enemies, often in the most aggressive ways, and readers today may be troubled by the violence of the romance and its insistent xenophobia. These, however, are characteristic of Middle English popular romance, and this genre is significant for the ways in which it enables the transformation of Richard's persona. As a literary genre, romance is adjacent to history in the Middle Ages. Whereas history attempts to tell things as they were, romance has the luxury of telling things as they could have been, as they ought to have been. Helen Cooper has trenchantly noted that 'history, as we know it, is romance written by the victors.'[33] The romancing of history in the *Richard Coeur de Lion* family of romances helps us to understand what a medieval English audience was looking for in a hero, and how fiction emerges from history. These are texts that expanded and changed over time, and which could

Château Gaillard, built by Richard to fortify the Duchy of Normandy;
where the romance stages his death.

be adapted to different requirements. Like Richard the Lionheart
himself, it is a romance that could rise to the occasion.

Many scholars have noted that the real Richard was larger
than life, and that truth is often stranger than fiction in his case.
This is the magic of *Richard Coeur de Lion*; it recasts the historical failure of the Third Crusade as the triumph of an English
king over his adversaries. Indeed, its significance to the literary
history of Richard the Lionheart lies in its casting of Richard
as a distinctly *English* hero, effacing the reality of his historical
position as the ruler of much of present-day France as well as
England, and relegating Richard's Christianity – the purported
purpose behind his crusade – to secondary importance. This
represents a significant reconceptualization of Richard, who,
during his lifetime, valued his French possessions as much as, if
not more than, his English ones, and whose primary identity
was probably linked to his status as duke of Aquitaine. He certainly would not have thought of himself as English in the way
that is imagined in *Richard Coeur de Lion*. In this regard the

romance plays a significant part in the establishment of Richard the Lionheart as the quintessential *English* king and hero. If you listen to stories about Richard, 'you shall hear of a bold man,/ A stout and skilful warrior,/ Whose heart was never found to be faint' (ll.6218–20).

FOUR

The Lionheart and
the Prince of Thieves

P erhaps the most significant and influential reader of the medieval romance *Richard Coeur de Lion* in terms of shaping the representation of Richard the Lionheart over the long term was the nineteenth-century Romantic novelist Sir Walter Scott. In the Introduction to his novel about Richard the Lionheart on crusade, *The Talisman* (1825), Scott notes his hesitancy to write about the East, given his lack of personal experience, then asserts that he is nevertheless confident in his sources:

> I had access to all which antiquity believed, whether of reality or fable, on the subject of that magnificent warrior, who was the proudest boast of Europe and their chivalry . . . The most curious register of the history of King Richard is an ancient romance, translated originally from the Norman; and at first certainly having a pretence to be termed a book of chivalry, but latterly becoming stuffed with the most astonishing and monstrous fables. There is perhaps no metrical romance on record where, along with curious and genuine history, are mingled more absurd and exaggerated incidents.[1]

In an Appendix Scott offers translations of the juiciest bits of the cannibalism scenes from *Richard Coeur de Lion*, along with some medieval analogues, taken from his friend George Ellis's *Specimens of Early English Metrical Romances* (1805).

Scott's interest in medieval romance developed early in his life, inspired in part by the Scottish folklore and balladry of his childhood, and in part by the fashion at the turn of the eighteenth century for the German Romantic poets. So taken was he by the romance of the past that as an adult he designed his house, Abbotsford, as a medieval manor. As a boy, one of Scott's favourite books had been Thomas Percy's *Reliques of Ancient English Poetry* (1765), a collection of medieval and early modern ballads and romances, including some about Sir Gawain, King Arthur and Robin Hood. The *Reliques* has a rather dramatic (and perhaps apocryphal) history; Percy claimed that he rescued an old medieval manuscript that his friend's maid had been using as kindling. Similarly, the Auchinleck Manuscript, which contains the earliest version of the *Richard Coeur de Lion* romance, and which Scott was able to borrow personally for several years for his own research, had been rescued from the possession of

Abbotsford House.

Robert Charles Bell, after John Watson Gordon, *Walter Scott*, 1871, engraving.

a professor who was using its parchment pages as notebook covers.

Borrowed plot elements from *Richard Coeur de Lion* are a recurring element of Scott's novels, including *Ivanhoe* (1819) and *The Talisman*, both of which take Richard as a main character.[2] Scott's novels, especially *Ivanhoe*, were hugely popular and influential, and they shaped popular perception of the medieval world for generations to come (so much so that the great Victorian historian E. A. Freeman felt forced to add an appendix to his magnum opus, *The History of the Norman Conquest of England* of 1867–79, debunking *Ivanhoe*). As a result, Scott also played an outsized role in shaping the literary legacy of Richard the Lionheart as it transitioned out of the Middle Ages and into modernity. One of the most influential ways in which he did this was to popularize the idea of a connection between Richard I and Robin Hood: two legendary figures of the Middle Ages, but two figures who had not always been connected and who had very different literary genealogies. Through Scott's influential work the two became intimately connected, inextricably linked in literature and legend, as Richard came increasingly to be associated with the legend of Robin Hood, and the Robin Hood legend came increasingly to centre on the theme of the struggle for justice in England in the absence of its crusader king. As this chapter will describe, this is a tradition that extends from the Middle Ages through the early novel to the age of cinema, and it is a connection to which much of the continued creativity and vitality of Richard the Lionheart's legend in the present day are owed.

At the same time that Scott was reading medieval romances, he was also corresponding with his friend the antiquary Joseph Ritson. Despite his day job as a lawyer, Ritson was enormously productive in compiling bibliographies and editions of medieval literature, mainly ballads and songs, but also romances. Although an irascible man, Ritson remained on good terms with Scott. His was the first scholarly edition of the late medieval Robin Hood ballads, *Robin Hood: A Collection of All the Ancient Poems Songs and Ballads Now Extant, Relative to that Celebrated Outlaw*, published in 1795. Ritson was convinced that Robin Hood was a historical figure, so he provided an introductory biography to his edition of the ballads. He believed that

> Robin Hood was born at Locksley, in the county of
> Nottingham, in the reign of King Henry the second,
> and about the year of Christ 1160. His extraction was
> noble, and his true name Robert Fitzooth, which vulgar
> pronunciation easily corrupted into Robin Hood. He is
> frequently styled, and commonly reputed to have been,
> Earl of Huntingdon.[3]

In the figure of Robin Hood Scott found another source of medieval inspiration: a rich vein of story elements and a yeoman foil to the Saxon and Norman aristocrats of *Ivanhoe*.

Despite the compelling fictions of *Ivanhoe* and *The Talisman*, the earliest Robin Hood ballads have no place for a King Richard. Although Roger of Howden reports that, upon his return from captivity in Germany, 'Richard, king of England, went to see Clipston and the forests of Sherwood, which he had never seen before, and they pleased him greatly,' this is the closest the historical Richard I would ever come to the legendary figure of Robin Hood.[4] The literature of the Robin Hood legend is capacious and sprawling, and, although it was clearly incredibly popular in the Middle Ages and Renaissance, it did not achieve a formalized, novelistic narrative until the nineteenth century. The earliest surviving texts are ballads from the very end of the fifteenth century. These introduce most of the cast of characters that are now familiar names: Robin Hood, Little John, the Sheriff of Nottingham, Guy of Gisborne. At the same time there was evidently a thriving, although now mostly lost, performance culture of Robin Hood plays and games, associated particularly with 'May Games' at Whitsun (Pentecost) and with charity collection. The Robin Hood ballads transitioned into print early. They were a popular topic in the broadside ballads of the seventeenth century (so called because they were printed on a single sheet of paper), whence they were gathered into themed collections, or

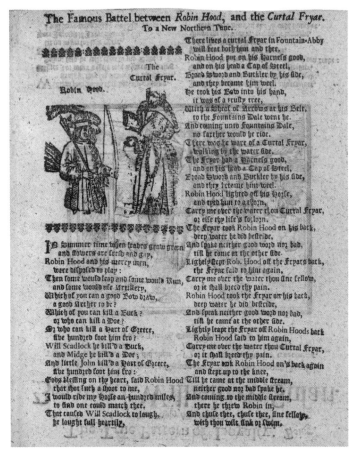

Robin Hood and the Curtail Friar, broadside ballad, 17th century.

'garlands', which thrived until the age of the novel, when many famous writers tilted at the windmill of the Robin Hood legend, including Dumas, Keats, Tennyson and, of course, Scott. In the nineteenth century the American Howard Pyle's *The Merry Adventures of Robin Hood* (1883) brought together many strands of the tradition, formalizing it into the stories that are most recognizable to readers today.

One of the earliest recorded Robin Hood ballads, 'Robin Hood and the Monk', pits Robin Hood against the Sheriff of

Nottingham for the robbery of a monk. Little John and Much the Miller's son set out to rescue Robin by killing the monk and tricking the king into surrendering instructions to the sheriff to release Robin into their custody. Instead of returning him to the king to face justice, as was the arrangement, Little John and Much secure Robin's release from imprisonment. The unnamed king, realizing he has been tricked, resolves ruefully to speak no more of the matter. In 'Robin Hood and the Potter', Robin is once again set against the sheriff. In this ballad he disguises himself as a potter and enters Nottingham to sell his pots at rock-bottom prices. This interests the sheriff's wife, so a disguised Robin dines at the sheriff's house and participates in an archery contest with the sheriff's men. Accepting the sheriff's request to lead him to Robin Hood, he instead leads the sheriff to his men in the forest and robs him, leaving the sheriff humiliated. As these two examples demonstrate, the earliest Robin Hood ballads are short and episodic, and they feature Robin's challenge to traditional forms of authority, be they monks, sheriffs or kings.[5]

The sixteenth-century *A Gest of Robyn Hode* comes closest to setting Robin Hood in proximity to royal authority. The *Gest* is much longer than the earlier ballads, and it weaves together earlier stories to create an overarching narrative of the life and times of Robin Hood. In it the Sheriff of Nottingham – failing to control the antics of Robin Hood and his companions – seeks the help of the king, who arrives in Nottingham only to be greeted by a six-month stand-off during which he rules in the city, but Robin rules in the forest. Finally, accepting that the only way to find Robin will be to meet him on his own grounds, the king disguises himself as an abbot with several of his knights as monks, and they enter the forest secure in the knowledge that Robin will be unable to resist robbing such a wealthy retinue. When the king (still disguised as an abbot) wins an archery contest and then, as his prize, gives Robin a mighty buffet, his disguise is blown and he is recognized as the king. The two men express mutual respect and the king invites Robin to join him at court, but Robin lasts only a year in this new environment before returning to his men in the greenwood. The relationship between Robin Hood, who declares 'I love no man in all the worlde/ So well As I do my kynge', and the king is not at all antagonistic.[6] Robin bows to royal authority, but at the same time the king envies Robin's natural authority and the unquestioning loyalty of his men. In *A Gest of Robyn Hode*, however, the king is named as 'Edwarde, our comly kynge'.[7]

The earliest writer to connect Robin Hood to Richard I, albeit only implicitly, was the Scottish chronicler John Major, who, in his *Historia Majoris Brittaniae* (1521), sets Robin's story in the 1190s. He writes:

> Around this time it was, as I conceive, that there
> flourished those most famous robbers Robert Hood,
> an Englishman, and Little John, who lay in wait in
> the woods but spoiled of their goods those only that
> were wealthy . . . The feats of this Robert were told
> in song all over Britain.[8]

It was also Major who introduced the idea, absent from the ballad tradition, that Robin Hood stole only from the rich and gave to the poor, and pronounced him 'the most humane and prince of all thieves'.[9] It was, however, Anthony Munday's plays *The Downfall of Robert, Earl of Huntingdon* and *The Death of Robert, Earl of Huntingdon* (both 1598) that first identified Robin Hood with the aristocratic 'Earl of Huntingdon', and which gave the legend the now familiar historical context. Robin Hood's adventures take place in the reign of King Richard I, while Richard is away on crusade. In the first of the two plays, in Richard's absence Robert's enemies, the Prior of St Mary's

Abbey and the Sheriff of Nottingham, contrive to have him outlawed for debt. Robert retreats to the forest and takes on the disguise of Robin Hood, a yeoman. He is joined there by his servants Little John and Much the Miller's son, and subsequently by two brothers whom he rescues from the sheriff's clutches, Scarlet and Scathlock. He is also joined by his lover, the aristocratic Matilda Fitzwater, who joins him in disguise as 'Maid Marian'. Ultimately, Robin's enemies also fall from grace and are forced to take refuge in the forest, where Robin finds them and graciously forgives them.[10]

The Downfall of Robert, Earl of Huntingdon fleshes out a biographical narrative for Robin Hood, explaining how he ended up an outlaw in the first place. This is a point that the medieval ballad tradition had been largely hesitant to address (although a seventeenth-century ballad, *Robin Hood's Progress to Nottingham*, portrays a fifteen-year-old Robin, who, when a group of foresters refuse to honour the bet they made on an archery contest, shoots and kills them all). In *The Downfall*, Munday attributes Robin's outlaw status to the plotting of his enemies, rather than to any fault of his own. Furthermore, by placing Robin's biography in the reign of Richard I, he situates Robin at a moment of political unrest, when good men might well be imagined to fall foul of competing power players. This historicizing of the Robin Hood legend changes its structure in consequential ways. Set in the frame of Richard's absence and return, Robin and Richard structurally occupy the same role: displaced from their natural position and under threat of being permanently barred from it. In this regard Robin represents on the microcosmic scale what Richard is to the macrocosmic. He can therefore operate as an outlaw while Richard is away, with the audience's full sympathy and seemingly without compromising law and order, which are in abeyance owing to the absence of the king. When Richard returns justice returns with him. So, whereas in the earlier tradition

Robin enjoyed the status of a first among equals in the greenwood, once he is firmly associated with Richard's reign he comes
to play a somewhat secondary role, while Richard emerges as
the true avatar of justice and right rule. This connection of
Richard to the Robin Hood tradition was compelling, and
Munday was one of the sources on which Ritson drew in his historicizing introduction to *Robin Hood: A Collection . . .*, treating
the fictional play as a true history.[11]

Scott, therefore, came to this narrative through his reading
of Ritson's edition, but he borrowed from it selectively in his
enormously popular novel *Ivanhoe*. This book tells the story of
its eponymous hero, Wilfred Ivanhoe, newly returned from
crusading with Richard the Lionheart, but returned in disguise
because he is estranged from his father, the Saxon Cedric of
Rotherwood. Cedric disapproves of Ivanhoe's decision to abandon his native England to follow a Norman king, and also of his
love for Cedric's ward, the beautiful Rowena. Rowena is of Saxon
royal blood, so Cedric hopes to marry her to Athelstane, the last
remaining Saxon heir to the English throne. Cedric chafes at the
subordination of the Saxon nobility to their new Norman over-
lords. When these three, along with the Jewish Isaac and his
daughter Rebecca, are captured by the Norman knight Maurice
de Bracy and the Templar Brian de Bois-Guilbert, a ragtag crew
of plucky Saxons (including the serfs Gurth and Wamba, Robin
Hood and Friar Tuck), along with a disguised Richard the Lionheart, band together to come to their rescue. Further adventures
ensue, including Rebecca being charged with witchcraft by the
Templars and rescued by Ivanhoe, who is reconciled to his father,
until Ivanhoe and Rowena are united in marriage, and Richard
casts off his disguise and is reunited with his kingdom.

Robin Hood plays only a supporting role in *Ivanhoe*, a novel
that paints an eloquent picture of the state of the nation in the
absence of Richard:

The condition of the English nation was at this time
sufficiently miserable. King Richard was absent a
prisoner, and in the power of the perfidious and cruel
Duke of Austria . . . To these causes of public distress
and apprehension, fall to be added the multitude of
outlaws who, driven to despair by the oppression of the
feudal nobility, and the severe exercise of the forest laws,
banded together in large gangs, and keeping possession
of the forests and the wastes, set at defiance the justice
and magistracy of the country.[12]

It is in this context that Robin Hood is introduced, here as a
yeoman called 'Locksley', a detail apparently borrowed from
Ritson. We find him standing up to a bullying Prince John and
agreeing to take part in an archery competition. Here, in a scene
taken from the medieval ballads, he distinguishes himself by
splitting the arrow of his opponent, demonstrating such skill
that even John is impressed. When the prince offers him employment, however, Locksley refuses, announcing: 'I have vowed,
that if I ever take service, it should be with your royal brother,
King Richard.'[13] And, indeed, Locksley and his companions fight
alongside the disguised King Richard until Cedric, Aethelstane
and Rowena are rescued and they finally reveal their identities
to one another. Upon hearing that Locksley is, in fact, 'Robin
Hood, of Sherwood Forest', Richard promptly pardons him:

'King of Outlaws, and Prince of Good Fellows!' said the
King, 'Who hath not heard a name that has been borne
as far as Palestine? Be assured, brave Outlaw, that no
deed done in our absence, and in the turbulent times
to which it has given rise, shall be remembered to thy
disadvantage.'[14]

The Robin Hood Scott presents in *Ivanhoe* recalls the Robin Hood of the medieval ballads: an archer, an outlaw and a yeoman. At the same time, however, the narrative represented in Munday's plays underlies the plot of *Ivanhoe*. The character of Ivanhoe himself takes on many of the characteristics of Munday's Robin Hood: a dispossessed nobleman, returned from crusade, loyal to the common cause, caught up in the politics of Prince John's misrule and restored to his rightful position with the return of King Richard.[15]

As for King Richard himself, when Richard the Lionheart first appears in the pages of *Ivanhoe*, at the tournament of Ashby-de-la-Zouch, he is all in black, an element borrowed from the tournament scene in *Richard Coeur de Lion*:

> There was among the ranks of the Disinherited Knight
> a champion in black armour, mounted on a black horse,
> large of size, tall, and to all appearance powerful and
> strong. This knight, who bore on his shield no device
> of any kind, had hitherto evinced very little interest
> in the event of the fight, beating off with seeming ease
> those knights who attacked him, but neither pursuing
> his advantages, nor himself assailing any one. In short,
> he acted the part rather of a spectator than of a party
> in the tournament, a circumstance which procured him
> among the spectators the name of *Le Noir Faineant*, or
> the Black Sluggard.[16]

This feigned lack of interest in all proceedings is as much part of Richard's disguise as his unmarked black armour. The disguise ensures also that Richard is introduced to the reader by his character before his true identity is revealed, and here he proves to be both noble and handsome. The unknown knight has thick, curly blond hair, sparkling blue eyes, red cheeks and a brawny physique.

He has 'altogether the look of a bold, daring and enterprising man'.[17] When he joins with the Saxons Gurth, Wamba, the friar and Robin Hood on the expedition to rescue Cedric, Rowena and the rest from their Norman captors, he is horrified to learn that the Normans have been acting as 'thieves and oppressors', and he identifies strongly as just the opposite: '"You can speak to no one," replied the knight, "to whom England, and the life of every Englishman, can be dearer than to me."'[18]

Richard's insistence that he is English, rather than identifying as Norman or Saxon, resolves the ethnic strife that the novel portrays as rending medieval society. The timeline suggested in *Ivanhoe*, as has long been noted, is patently absurd: characters, and their fathers, are depicted as having fought with the last English king, an impossibility given the hundred-year time lapse between the Norman Conquest of 1066 and the novel's setting in the late twelfth century. Indeed, four Norman kings reigned in England between the time of William the Conqueror and Richard the Lionheart. Nevertheless, Richard is situated as a figure who rises above these ethnic partisan allegiances, embodying the best of both, although he consistently fights on the side of the Saxons against the Normans, implying that these are the true 'English'. When he participates in the storming of the Castle of Torquilstone, his war cry is 'Saint George for England!', while the Norman defenders urge one another on by name in French, and he rallies his troops by referring to their 'true English hearts'.[19]

Nevertheless, *Ivanhoe* expresses misgivings about Richard as a king, even at the moment in which he drops his disguise and reassumes his identity as king of England. These misgivings are foregrounded in the somewhat absurd nickname Scott gives Richard, 'The Black Sluggard'. As Robin Hood leads Richard and Ivanhoe to a banquet in the woods with his companions, the narrator takes a moment to reflect upon Richard:

Novelty in society and in adventure was the zest of life to Richard Coeur de Lion, and it had its highest relish when enhanced by dangers encountered and surmounted. In the lion-hearted King, the brilliant, but useless character, of a knight of romance, was in great measure realized; and the personal glory which he acquired by his own deeds of arms, was far more dear to his excited imagination than that which a course of policy and wisdom would have spread around his government. Accordingly, his reign was like the course of a brilliant and rapid meteor, which shoots along the face of heaven, shedding around an unnecessary and portentous light, which is instantly swallowed up by universal darkness; his feats of chivalry furnishing themes for bards and minstrels, but affording none of those solid benefits to his country on which history loves to pause, and hold up as an example to posterity. But in his present company, Richard shewed to the greatest imaginable advantage. He was gay, good-humoured, liberal, and fond of manhood in every rank of life.[20]

This assessment of Richard's character, as 'brilliant but useless', is followed shortly by an even more damning assessment of his reign. Richard, the narrator tells us, is popular 'by his personal good qualities and military fame', but 'his administration was wilfully careless, now too indulgent, and now allied to despotism.'[21]

This mixed assessment of the king's character is echoed in *The Talisman*, which is set in the years prior to *Ivanhoe*, during Richard's crusade. *The Talisman* gestures to the earlier novel with an intertextual reference to Robin Hood: 'We have heard of late,' says Sir Kenneth,

by minstrels and pilgrims, that your outlawed yeomen have formed great bands in the shires of York and

Nottingham, having at their head a most stout archer,
called Robin Hood, with his lieutenant, Little John.
Methinks it were better that Richard relaxed his
forest-code in England, than tried to enforce it in
the Holy Land.[22]

The trouble back in England is reflected by the strife among
the crusaders. As does the medieval romance *Richard Coeur de
Lion*, *The Talisman* revisits the historical scene of Richard's siege
of Acre in 1191, when he was struck down by illness. Unlike the
plot of *Richard Coeur de Lion*, however, in Scott's novel Richard
is healed by no other than Saladin, who comes to him in disguise
as a doctor, brought by the novel's hero Sir Kenneth, the Knight
of the Couchant Leopard. Sir Kenneth is similarly in disguise,
since he is in truth David, Earl of Huntingdon (and thus the
holder of the title Scott removed from his Robin Hood), heir to
the throne of Scotland. Sir Kenneth fights in disguise to prove
his worth, but also to conceal his hopeless love for Richard's
niece Edith. The novel portrays infighting and intrigue within
the crusader camp, while the two outsiders, the Scottish Kenneth
and the Muslim Saladin, are portrayed as equally exemplary in
their sense of honour and nobility. The representation of Richard
shares this heightened sense of honour. The respect in which he
is held by those loyal to him is unquestioned. The novel portrays
Richard as bold and valiant, to be sure, but at the same time he
is depicted as his own worst enemy. The difficulties of crusade
are described as

> in a great measure, counter-balanced by the stern
> resolution and restless activity of King Richard who,
> with some of his best knights, was ever on horseback,
> ready to repair to any point where danger occurred,
> and often, not only bringing unexpected succour to

the Christians, but discomforting the infidels when
they seemed most secure of victory.[23]

At the same time, however, Richard is portrayed as 'Naturally rash
and impetuous, the irritability of his temper preyed on itself'.[24]

While these descriptions of Richard as a less than ideal ruler
may seem to contradict the representation of him as a chivalric
hero, in fact they accurately reflect a shift in public opinion of
him in the eighteenth and nineteenth centuries. Throughout the
Middle Ages Richard's reputation remained high. An often quoted
remark from the fourteenth-century chronicler Ranulf Higden
says that the English boasted of Richard in the same way that the
French boasted of Charlemagne, or the Greeks of Alexander.[25]
This high estimation of Richard continued into the Renaissance,
and in Shakespeare's play *The Life and Death of King John*, Richard
is remembered as a great hero: 'that robb'd the lion of his heart/
And fought the holy wars in Palestine' (ii.i.3–4).

As early as 1621, however, the historian Samuel Daniel
wrote that Richard

> exacted and consumed more of this kingdom than all
> his predecessors from the Normans had done before
> him, and yet deserved less of any, having neither lived
> here, neither left behind him any monument of piety
> or of any other public work, or ever showed love or
> care to this Commonwealth, but only to get what he
> could from it.[26]

Although initially this was a dissenting opinion, over time it
gained traction. By the end of the eighteenth century the tide
of opinion had turned decisively. Richard's famous joke – that
he would sell London if he could only find a buyer – had not
aged well. He was judged increasingly by historians for the sin

of favouring his French lands over England, and for having spent little time in the latter country. Following the assessment of such historians as David Hume, in his widely read *History of England* (1754–62), the great Victorian historian William Stubbs described Richard as 'a selfish ruler and a vicious man'.[27] Walter Scott himself in *Ivanhoe* cites the Revd Dr Robert Henry's *The History of Great Britain, from the Invasions of It by the Romans under Julius Caesar* (1777–93): 'to prove that fiction itself can hardly reach the dark reality of the horrors of the period'.[28] In Henry's final estimation, although Richard was celebrated by his contemporaries,

> This prince was not so eminent for his virtues as for
> his accomplishments. On the contrary, though on
> some occasions he acted in a noble manner, especially
> to his prostrate enemies, he was in general haughty, cruel,
> covetous, passionate, and sensual, an undutiful son, an
> unfaithful husband, and a most pernicious king, having,
> by his long absence and continual wars, drained his
> English dominions of both men and money.[29]

It is precisely out of this contradiction – the representation of Richard as a heroic warrior alongside his representation as a bad king – that the association of Richard as a figure for right rule emerges in the literary tradition, and comes to dominate all subsequent literary representations of him. This association emerges with particular clarity in the connection of Richard the Lionheart with the Robin Hood tradition, and it is inflected by this reassessment of Richard's reign. The narrative that Scott popularizes – of the troubles of England in the absence of her crusading king – provides a useful and durable framework for reconsiderations of both the nature of just rule and the value of crusade.

In the Robin Hood tradition Richard the Lionheart and
Robin Hood came to develop a symbiotic relationship. Richard's
entanglement with the Robin Hood legend helped to keep the
myth of Richard the Lionheart alive, but at the same time the
representation of Richard as a crusader in particular enabled
the Robin Hood tradition to do a new kind of cultural work as it
emerged into modernity. This symbiosis is particularly evident
in the cinematic versions of Robin Hood that come to form some
of its most iconic instantiations in the present day. Some classic
film versions, such as *The Adventures of Robin Hood* (1938),
simply present the problem as one of bad governance enabled
by the absent king. Here the story is framed by the absence and
return of the king, whose simple presence unifies his subjects
and restores justice to his kingdom. Scenes from the medieval
and early modern ballad tradition – among them the competition
for the golden arrow, the fight with Little John over the river, and
shooting the garlands – are folded within this new narrative that
reframes their meaning. The reason Richard has been absent from
England, however, is that he has been on crusade. In these versions, not only is Richard's crusading called into question, but
also Robin Hood himself is cast as a – disenchanted – crusader.

The idea that Robin should himself accompany Richard
the Lionheart on crusade is no part of the medieval tradition,
but once Scott had popularized the connection between Richard
and Robin, the importance of crusading to Richard's mythos
soon enveloped Robin Hood as well. J. H. Stocqueler's novel *Maid
Marian: The Forest Queen* (1849), for example, seizes on Robin's
unique skill and sends him on crusade with Richard as an archer.
The popular comic opera *Maid Marian* (1901), by Harry B. Smith
and Reginald De Koven, also presents Robin as a crusader, although Richard himself is entirely absent from the story; his
structural role is largely usurped by Robin himself, whose absence
allows the sheriff and Guy of Gisborne to plot against him and

whose subsequent return after escaping a kidnapping restores order. It was, however, the silent film *Robin Hood* (1922, dir. Allan Dwan), starring Douglas Fairbanks in the title role, that solidified the representation of Robin Hood as a crusader in the popular imagination, and which gave Richard the Lionheart an outsized role in the story. One critic has noted that 'In both form and content, it marks a transition between the nineteenth-century literary and twentieth-century film worlds.'[30] Richard the Lionheart plays a much greater role in this adaptation of the legend than in most subsequent film adaptations of the Robin Hood material, being absent on crusade only for the second half of the action. Indeed, at the heart of the film is Robin's – here the Earl of Huntingdon – relationship with the king, which takes up the first half.

The film opens with extravagant scenes of medieval pageantry as Richard attends a tournament celebrating his imminent departure on crusade. Whereas the huge set mostly dwarfs the figures within it, in these scenes Richard himself is large, shown in close-up, and in charismatic contrast to his somewhat effeminate brother Prince John, who is described as 'sinister' and 'dour'. Huntingdon's performance at the tournament wins him the role of Richard's second-in-command on crusade. Fairbanks's Robin Hood displays an unproblematic relationship with crusading, and Richard's crusade is itself an absent presence at the heart of the film. Although it is the lynchpin of the plot, enabling Prince John's terrorizing of the population, the crusade is represented visually by a single title card announcing its end – 'In far-off Palestine Richard meets with victory and concludes a truce with the infidel' – and a scene in which a mounted Richard oversees a procession of 'infidel' soldiers exiting a fortified city. Thus even when Richard is off-screen his return is felt to be imminent.

The treatment of crusade here is not political but personal, the occasion of a breakdown of trust between the two men. When

Marian writes to Robin about John's predations, Robin determines to conceal the reason for his return to England from Richard, fearing that concern for his kingdom will cause the king to abandon the crusade. The king, who had previously encouraged the reluctant Robin to court Marian, now accuses him of turning 'chicken-hearted for a wench'. The misunderstanding is completed when Guy of Gisborne, who himself hopes to take Robin's place as Richard's lieutenant, prevents Robin from telling the truth and instead shows Richard a letter from Robin to Marian which he has intercepted, and which seemingly confirms Richard's suspicions that Robin is deserting him for Marian. Nevertheless, Richard cannot bring himself to have Robin executed for treason as Guy suggests, and for his part Robin seems to ignore Richard's bad faith completely, escaping from prison and returning to England to defend Richard's interests in his absence. The film's theme, therefore, is about finding a balance between the overly homosocial behaviour that Robin displays at the beginning and becoming too feminized by the company of women. Throughout, Richard himself exemplifies this balance. The film steers clear of the nationalizing and political themes that dominated subsequent film adaptations of the Robin Hood legend.

The classic treatment of Robin Hood on the silver screen is without doubt *The Adventures of Robin Hood* (1938, dir. Michael Curtiz and William Keighley), starring Errol Flynn. The film opens with a title card that links it back to the 1922 version: 'In the year of Our Lord 1191 when Richard, the Lion-Heart, set forth to drive the infidels from the Holy Land, he gave the Regency of his kingdom to his trusted friend, Longchamps, instead of to his treasonous brother, King John.' The next card lays out the antagonism between Norman and Saxon: 'Bitterly resentful, John hoped for some disaster to befall Richard so that he, with the help of the Norman barons, might seize the throne for himself. And then on a luckless day for the Saxons . . .' The debt to *Ivanhoe* is clear and, unlike in the 1922 film, there is no suggestion that Robin joins Richard on crusade.

The action opens with the town crier announcing the misfortune: King Richard has been captured and is being held captive by Leopold of Austria. Thus the scenario is set, and the first scene finds Much the Miller's son caught poaching. When challenged by Sir Guy of Gisborne (a rakishly handsome Basil Rathbone), Much exclaims: 'When King Richard escapes, he'll . . .' (the sentence is left to trail off impotently). The problem of Richard's absence is thus articulated twice: announced extra-diegetically and experienced diegetically. In the interim, Robin Hood makes a plea to 'free-born Englishmen' – implicitly, that is, all Englishmen – to join him in resisting the twin evils of Sir Guy and Prince John, who plots the murders of both Robin and Richard. The ethnic drama of Norman vs Saxon is played out across the character of Marian, a Norman noblewoman who initially despises the Saxons, but comes to support their cause, exclaiming, 'England is bigger than just Norman and Saxon.' Marian, although Norman, echoes Scott's representation of Ivanhoe as a character able to bridge the ethnic divide. When Richard does return, he arrives in disguise as a common man. In a scene borrowed from the medieval ballad *A Gest of Robyn Hode*, he attracts Robin by dressing as a monk, ripe for robbing. He tests the devotion of Robin, who asserts of Richard that 'his task was here at home defending his own people instead of deserting them to fight in foreign lands.' In the event, Richard banishes the evil Prince John, restores Robin Hood to his lands and, indeed, elevates him to an earldom, and, perhaps most importantly, unites Normans and Saxons into Englishmen. The film thus ends with Richard reasserting his authority over a realm in which, as he announces, 'Normans and Saxons alike will share the rights of Englishmen.'

To be sure, *The Adventures of Robin Hood* engages more deeply with politics than just with the imagined Saxon–Norman

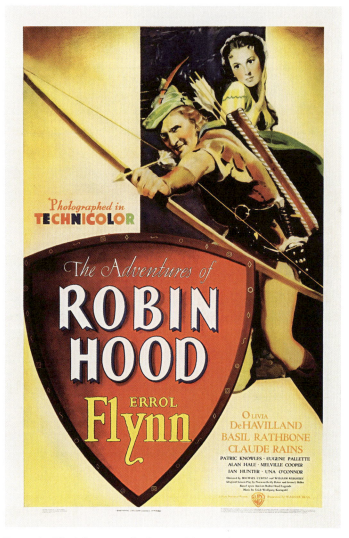

Poster for *The Adventures of Robin Hood* (1938, dir. Michael Curtiz and William Keighley).

antagonism inherited from Scott. Critics have noted that Robin Hood's anti-war sentiment should be read in the context of American anxiety about becoming embroiled in the political unrest that was shaking Europe at the end of the 1940s. The film echoes Scott's conservatism in this regard, suggesting that political injustice can be traced to bad rulers rather than bad systems. Thus, in these earliest Robin Hood films, crusading is presented as a problem only insofar as it is the cause of the king's absence. Richard tends to arrive at the end of the story as a *deus ex machina* who restores justice to Robin Hood and also to the English people, for whom Robin stands in metonymically. Increasingly, however, more recent films – among them *Robin and Marian* (1976, dir. Richard Lester), *Robin Hood: Prince of Thieves* (1991, dir. Kevin Reynolds), *Robin Hood* (2010, dir. Ridley Scott) and *Robin Hood* (2018, dir. Otto Bathurst) – use the representation of Richard's crusading to register more contemporary cultural concerns about the policy of Western powers in the Middle East. Through the ambivalent representation of Richard's crusades alongside that of Robin Hood as a disenchanted crusader, these cinematic adaptations offer a limited critique of contemporary wars in the Middle East while at the same time underwriting the ideology that maintains them.

Thus, for example, *Robin and Marian* is unique in the tradition of Robin Hood adaptations in that it imagines Robin in old age. Here, Robin, played by Sean Connery, has left Sherwood and Marian (played by Audrey Hepburn) behind to follow Richard on crusade. At least, Little John comments, he *almost* got to see Jerusalem. But the crusade is long over and Richard now seems a faithless and capricious king, who fights for treasure rather than for God. The opening scenes of the film find an older Robin and Little John in a dry, barren landscape with a small band of men haplessly laying siege to a half-ruined castle. King Richard arrives at this dismal scene and orders Robin to destroy the castle and everyone in it. When Robin refuses, protesting that only women and children remain ('I followed you for twenty years. I fought for you on the crusades, I fought for you here in France. Show me a soldier and I'll fight him now. But I won't slaughter children for a piece of gold that never was'), Richard has them arrested and reduces the castle himself – but not before an elderly man (seemingly the castle's only defender) throws an arrow that wounds Richard fatally in the neck. With these opening scenes, *Robin and Marian* plays off the legendary stories that accrued to Richard's death at the siege of Châlus-Chabrol: that Richard was seeking treasure, not honour, and that his death was caused by an arrow wound that turned gangrenous. Richard's absence, so often thematized in the Robin Hood tradition, is now permanent. *Robin and Marian* offers a more cynical take on Richard's character and his legacy. Here, the crusade is a distant memory, and although it is not criticized as such, it is clear that the adventure has brought no lasting glory or reward.

Ridley Scott's *Robin Hood*, starring Russell Crowe in the title role, opens with the same scene: the Siege of Châlus-Chabron. This time, however, the personal has become political. The plot of this version departs from tradition entirely, telling of Robin returning to England from the crusades in order to foil a French invasion. The importance of Robin Hood as a crusader has taken over from the importance of Richard as an absent king, and the commentary on just rule is now aimed squarely at contemporary Middle Eastern politics. The scene at Châlus-Chabron is set by a title card: 'King Richard the Lion Heart, bankrupt of wealth and glory, is plundering his way back to England after ten years on his Crusade.' When Richard wanders around his army's camp at night, he is caught up in a brawl between Robin and another soldier over a game of chance. Finding Robin to be an honest man when he confesses to having thrown the first punch, and seeking a change from the flattery of his closest companion, Richard asks Robin: 'What's your opinion of my crusade? Will God be pleased with my sacrifice?' Robin replies in the negative, specifically because of Richard's massacre of Muslim prisoners after the fall of Acre. Robin's honesty lands him and his companions in the stocks, awaiting whipping, branding and perhaps hanging, until Richard's death by arrow at the siege provides the opportunity for their escape.

Perhaps the most extended use in the Robin Hood tradition of Richard the Lionheart's crusade is that of *Robin Hood: Prince of Thieves*, starring Kevin Costner as Robin Hood. This adaptation maintains the tradition of announcing King Richard's absence in a title card: '800 years ago, Richard "The Lionheart", King of England, led the third Great Crusade to reclaim the Holy Land from the Turks.' As in the film of 1938, Richard's absence enables the rapacity of lesser authority figures with treasonous ambitions. *Robin Hood: Prince of Thieves* abandons the character of Prince John and instead focuses all these treasonous ambitions in the figure of the Sheriff of Nottingham. Produced in the shadow of the First Gulf War, it follows the announcement of Richard's crusade with a reminder of the costs of war: 'Most of the young English noblemen who flocked to his banner never returned home.' The film then opens in 'Jerusalem 1194 AD', with the sun setting on the call to prayer from a minaret. From this peaceful scene, we are transported immediately to a torture chamber, where the hands of crusaders falsely accused of stealing are being chopped off, in a not-so-subtle reference to the debate over the cruelty of (largely misunderstood) Sharia law in justifying the First Gulf War. 'Show them the courage of Allah,' a bearded and turbaned man who seems to be the head torturer, taunts his unlucky victim.

In contrast to these torturers, however, is the character of Azeem, played by Morgan Freeman: also a Muslim, but also a prisoner.[31] Azeem helps Robin Hood to escape the prison and becomes his sidekick as Robin travels home to England, where he will defeat the sheriff, marry Marian and thus preserve the kingdom for Richard. The character of Azeem – loyal, noble, civilized, devout – is evidently intended to provide an enlightened representation of Muslims. His use of technology, particularly that of warfare, is more advanced than that of the English, even as his trademark weapon is a large scimitar. The figure of Azeem is woven through the film as a constant reminder of the crusading context, and as a constant neo-liberal plea for tolerance. When Robin gives his rousing speech to the Merry Men urging them to fight for their freedoms, he notes soberly, while looking meaningfully at Azeem, that 'one free man defending his home is more powerful than ten hired soldiers; the crusades taught me that.'

With its representation of the Third Crusade, *Robin Hood: Prince of Thieves* wants to have it both ways. On the one hand, brutal, barbaric Muslims run a torture chamber of horrors, taunting their victims in the name of Allah, while on the other is the profoundly Orientalizing representation of Azeem, the purveyor of advanced (and, for the twelfth century, anachronistic) technology, yet bound by a traditional vow to repay the 'debt' incurred when Robin saved his life. Here there are only two kinds of Muslim: those who torture Westerners and those who serve them. As Edward Said described so influentially in his seminal work, *Orientalism* (1978), 'the Orient is at bottom something either to be feared . . . or to be controlled.'[32] The fact that the crusades were wars of Western aggression is not admitted by this dungeon scene, where the captive crusaders appear only as victims. As a crusader, Robin Hood's violence is justified by the cruelty of his jailers.

These two stereotypes of the Muslim are differentiated by skin colour, since Azeem is played by an African-American actor. The film's representation of religious difference is thereby racialized ('whatever blood is in your veins, no one deserves to die in there,' Robin tells Azeem as they escape) and sutured on to a peculiarly American multiculturalism (his skin is a different colour, Azeem tells an impertinent little English girl, because 'Allah loves wondrous variety'). Indeed, when Robin addresses the people of Sherwood at the Gallows Oak, the crowd is entirely white; in this scene, Englishness is imagined as whiteness. Thus, as Matthew

Schlimm has written of the crusade film *Kingdom of Heaven* (2005), the film 'preaches a message of tolerance while ironically embodying forms of neocolonialism and Orientalism'.[33] However, although the action of the film is framed by Richard's absence and return (to give Marian away at her wedding to Robin), the costs of crusading are separated from the figure of the crusading king, who is represented as unproblematically heroic. When Richard returns, he mentions only the near loss of his kingdom, not the loss of his crusade.

By the time of the 2018 *Robin Hood*, starring Taron Egerton, the association between Robin and the critique of crusading had been made so thoroughly through the figure of Richard the Lionheart that Richard appears nowhere in the film; the role of villain is now assigned solely to the Sheriff of Nottingham. The film, which is cast as an 'origin story' for Robin Hood, opens with the aristocratic Lord Robin of Loxley receiving a 'draft notice' that he is called up for the crusade. This anachronism is stunningly extended into the opening scenes of battle, which mimic scenes from the contemporary wars in the Middle East, only with the soldiers using bows and arrows.[34] As one reviewer described, 'An opening action sequence set in Syria has stuttering handheld camerawork in the vein of *Saving Private Ryan* and *Black Hawk Down*.'[35] The setting could just as soon be Fallujah in 2004 as Acre in 1191. When Robin fails to prevent his commanding officer, Guy of Gisborne, from executing prisoners, he abandons the crusade and returns to an England seemingly governed by the Sheriff of Nottingham. The sheriff, it is revealed, is in cahoots with the Church, which is funding both sides of the crusades in an effort to overthrow the king and claim power. If the critique of contemporary geopolitics in the battle scenes were not clear, the sheriff mouths such post-9/11 propaganda as 'they hate us for our freedom' and intimates that the Muslim threat will soon endanger the homeland ('they'll burn your houses!'). Following the tradition of *Robin Hood: Prince of Thieves*, Robin returns from his crusade with a Muslim companion, played again by an African-American actor, Jamie Foxx, who becomes Little John, an older and wiser mentor figure. As sidekicks to the disenchanted crusader that is the postmodern Robin Hood, these characters seem, on the surface, to offer a plea for multiculturalism and a kind of colour-blind politics. We are all the same under the skin, they seem to suggest; or, as Azeem says, 'Allah loves wondrous variety.' In these films, however, Azeem and Little John remain sidekicks. We have yet, after all, to see a Black Robin Hood. The tolerance they preach is at odds with the continued Western military presence in the Middle East and with continued structural racism in the United States and elsewhere.

In this regard, the return of Richard the Lionheart represents a return to the status quo. The carnivalesque experiments with freedom and equality that we see in the greenwood can be safely contained within the old world order of aristocratic white male governance. A striking aspect of both the 2010 (Russell Crowe) and 2018 (Taron Egerton) adaptations is that without the possibility of Richard's return to re-establish justice in his kingdom – the former version begins with his death and the latter never mentions him at all – justice is simply not restored. The ending of both adaptations sees Robin Hood retreat to the forest with his merry men, to regroup and return to fight another day. The ending of the 2010 version, for example, features a voice-over by Maid Marian, describing their 'new life in the greenwood, noting that they live in equality' as they continue to fight on the side of right against the treacherous King John. This notion of the greenwood as a self-governing socialist utopia is even more pronounced in the 2018 version. Here the Sheriff of Nottingham has sent the townspeople to work in a coal mine. Will Scarlett emerges as the leader of the miners, who are plotting to rise up and overthrow the sheriff. In this he resembles nothing more than a labour union leader. In the end, however, the popular uprising fails and Robin, Little John and Marian flee to Sherwood Forest, along with the commoners whose rebellion has been mostly unsuccessful. There they share out the loot they have stolen from the sheriff, in a sign that this, too, will be a utopian society, rejecting the false consolations of sovereignty.

Like the novels of Walter Scott, these cinematic versions of the Robin Hood legend present a conflicted view of Richard's character and rule. This is a paradox of the legacy of Scott's novels. On the one hand, their enormous popularity ensured that the figure of Richard the Lionheart remained central to the English literary imagination. On the other, Scott's yoking together of the legends of Richard and Robin means that much of the time Richard's presence paradoxically depends on his absence. Nevertheless, as with the medieval ballads and Scott's novels, films are designed as popular entertainment. The cinematic tradition of Robin Hood films continues to keep Richard the Lionheart at the forefront of the popular imagination.

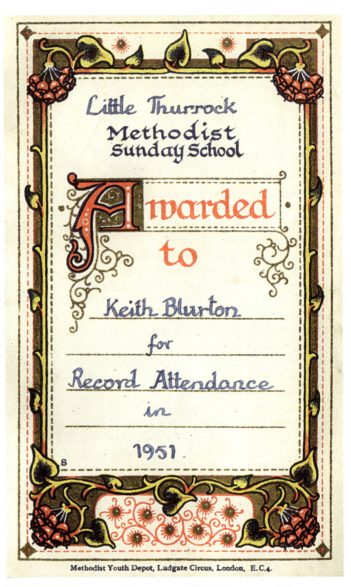

Little Thurrock
Methodist
Sunday School

Awarded
to

Keith Blurton

for

Record Attendance

in

1951

Methodist Youth Depot, Ludgate Circus, London, E.C.4.

Printed bookplate inserted in a copy of *The Talisman* awarded
to Keith Blurton, the author's father, for record attendance
at the Little Thurrock Methodist Sunday School, 1951.

Epilogue

In 1951, in the industrial area of Grays Thurrock in southeastern England, my father was given a copy of *The Talisman* for perfect attendance at Sunday School. By that time the presentation of Walter Scott's novel of Richard the Lionheart on the Third Crusade to an eleven-year-old boy made a profound kind of cultural sense. The story of the legend of Richard the Lionheart between the Middle Ages and the modern era is largely one of Richard becoming associated with a strong sense of an English nationalism. This nationalism is deeply inflected by an ethos of chivalric behaviour imagined to characterize the English character. Such representations have their root in the Middle Ages. Richard I was entering into legend even in his own lifetime. 'The head and father of valour, the mighty and valiant Richard, king of the English', the troubadour Gaucelm Faidit calls him, and Gaucelm was by no means alone in this opinion.[1] A significant aspect of Richard's apotheosis is the way in which, beginning in the fourteenth century with the earliest version of the *Richard Coeur de Lion* romance, Richard came to be seen not just as a legendary king, but as a quintessentially *English* king. As the romance insists, people want to know about King Richard and other 'valiant knights of England'.[2] And in Richard's escapades on crusade he is identified as much as an English crusader as a Christian one; the romance identifies Richard's followers as 'English Christian' men.[3] While during the Middle Ages Richard was regarded as an excellent king (with the possible exception of one thirteenth-century bishop, who opined that it took 33 years in Purgatory to cleanse Richard's soul), the reassessments of his reign that began as early as the sixteenth century contested it precisely on this ground: the extent to which he was felt to value England appropriately.[4]

Nevertheless, at the same time that Victorian historians such as William Stubbs were criticizing Richard ('a selfish ruler and a vicious man'), the memory of Richard was intersecting with the emergence of medievalism as a cultural force in England.[5] By 'medievalism', I mean the rebirth of interest in the Middle Ages that encompassed literature, art and architecture, and which took creative inspiration from engagement with the medieval past. The novels of Scott, including *Ivanhoe* and *The Talisman*, are but one example of this. Another is the famous Eglinton Tournament of 1839: a re-creation of a medieval tournament, in which aristocratic men dressed up in (purportedly) medieval suits of armour and faced one another on the jousting field. The joust itself, as well as its honouring of 'The Queen of Beauty', was modelled on the Tournament of Ashby-de-la-Zouch in *Ivanhoe*. The famous statue of Richard I that now stands outside the Houses of Parliament, created by the Italian sculptor Carlo Marochetti for the Great Exhibition of 1851, so impressed Queen Victoria and Prince Albert that they organized a fund to install the statue in its current location. The architecture of the Houses of Parliament itself is the result of this culture of medievalism, rebuilt over the course of the second half of the nineteenth century in the Gothic Revival style to look transparently medieval.

Another aspect of this engagement with the medieval past was the effort of retrieval of the literature of the Middle Ages, seen in the scholarship of Scott's friends and colleagues Joseph Ritson and George Ellis. It was also during this period that the medieval chroniclers described in Chapter One began to be edited and printed: Roger of Howden, for example, in 1853, and Richard of Devizes in 1884. Similarly inspired by nineteenth-century medievalism is the only previous book to describe the literary legacy of Richard I: George Henry Needler's dissertation *Richard Coeur de Lion in Literature* (1890). The opening lines of this study read:

> The Life of Richard Coeur de Lion fell in the midst of a
> period in which, more than any other in the history of
> Western Europe, men gave themselves up to the delights
> of adventure and the sturdy joys of living; when, more
> than at any other time, life was made a romance.[6]

This description is in a sense the obverse of Scott's assessment of Richard's character: 'In the lion-hearted King, the brilliant, but useless character, of a knight of romance, was in great measure realized.'[7]

Needler's idea of 'life . . . made a romance' resonated for many in the nineteenth century. The adventurous spirit of the crusades seemed to offer a forerunner of the spirit of nineteenth-century English imperialism. The crusades offered the ideal opportunity for the display of English chivalry, a concept that was becoming

Joust at the Eglinton Tournament of 1839.

more and more associated with a code of conduct appropriate to the present as much as to the past. Scott defined the concept in his 'Essay on Chivalry' (1815–24), originally written for the *Encyclopaedia Britannica*:

> Generosity, gallantry, and an unblemished reputation were no less necessary ingredients in the character of a perfect knight. He was not called upon simply to practise these virtues when opportunity offered, but to be sedulous and unwearied in searching for the means of exercising them, and to push them without hesitation to the brink of extravagance, or even beyond it.[8]

Indeed, in the words of the historian Mark Girouard, 'By the end of the nineteenth century a gentleman had to be chivalrous, or at least if he were not he was not fully a gentleman.'[9] In this context the literary example of Richard the Lionheart played a significant role in modelling how a chivalrous gentleman should act. Adventure stories for boys, in particular, often focused on a narrative formula in which a young boy might follow Richard on crusade and win renown and glory through the exercise of feats of valour and chivalrous behaviour.[10] In his bestselling *Scouting for Boys* (1908), the British army officer and founder of the Boy Scouts Robert Baden-Powell extols Richard as a prototype boy scout: one of the 'real men' who 'give up everything, their personal comforts and desires, in order to get their work done. They do not do this for their own amusement, but because it is their duty to their king, fellow-countrymen, or employers.'[11] Baden-Powell presents Richard the Lionheart as a quintessential example of self-sacrifice: 'King Richard I, who was one of the first Scouts of Empire, left his kingdom, his family, and everything to go and fight against the enemies of the Christian religion,' and he recommends Scott's *The Talisman* to his reader.[12]

Lead casket containing Richard I's embalmed heart.

It was also during this new craze for all things medieval in the early nineteenth century that Richard the Lionheart's embalmed heart was discovered in a lead box during archaeological excavations in Rouen Cathedral in 1838. As was common for medieval kings, Richard's mortal remains had been dispersed throughout his territories. Roger of Howden describes Richard on his deathbed making his wishes known: 'The king then gave orders that his brains, his blood, and his entrails should be buried at Châlus, his heart at Rouen, and his body at Fontevraud, at the feet of his father.'[13] Although the story of Richard's death seems a fittingly dramatic end for this larger-than-life king, it

Effigy of Richard I, Fontevraud Abbey.

has not brought an end to the telling and retelling of his story. Struck down by a single arrow as he casually walked out to survey the siege of Châlus-Chabrol without first putting on his armour, Richard has nonetheless never seemed far from the cultural imaginary. As early as the thirteenth century, the verse biography of the famous knight William the Marshall suggests that the fatal arrow had been poisoned: '[Richard] went and laid siege to Nontron; but he hadn't been there long before a Satan, a traitor, a minister of the devil, loosed from the battlement a poisoned bolt, inflicting a wound on the finest prince on earth that he was bound to die, to the grievous cost of all the world.'[14]

Of course it would come as no surprise that it should take a poisoned arrow to dispatch a lion's heart, and the legend of the poisoned arrow persisted, to be finally laid to rest only in 2013, when a team of French researchers put Richard's heart to a 'full biomedical analysis'. They were interested in the science of medieval embalming, and, among other discoveries, they found that Richard's heart had been embalmed with the very highest-quality herbs and spices, including frankincense. The use of frankincense, which may have been intended to confer the odour of sanctity, suggests that medieval embalmers were equally interested in the science and the theology of embalming.[15] Unfortunately for the conspiratorially minded, the team found no evidence of poison. While Richard's fatal final wound was not, then, the spectacular act of a traitorous poison, the continued interest in the life and death of Richard the Lionheart, even extending to the pages of scientific journals, nevertheless gestures to its capacity for renewal, and to the continuing purchase of the legend of Richard the Lionheart on our cultural imagination.

CHRONOLOGY

8 September 1157	Richard I of England is born
1172	Richard invested as duke of Aquitaine and count of Poitou
1173	Richard joins his brothers Henry and Geoffrey in rebellion against their father, Henry II
1179	Richard joins his father, Henry II, against his brothers Henry and Geoffrey
11 June 1183	Richard's brother Henry dies, making him the heir presumptive
19 August 1186	Richard's brother Geoffrey, count of Brittany, dies
1186–9	Richard joins his younger brother John and King Philip II of France in rebellion against his father, Henry II
1187	Saladin captures Jerusalem at the Battle of Hattin; Richard takes the cross
1188	In November Richard pays homage to King Philip II of France for his French possessions
1189	Death of King Henry II. Richard invested as duke of Normandy (20 July) and becomes king
13 September 1189	Coronation of Richard I in Westminster Abbey
1189–92	The Third Crusade
5 December 1189	The signing of the Quitclaim of Canterbury gives William I of Scotland independence from the English Crown
March 1190	Massacre of the Jews at York
1190	Richard sets off on crusade, leaving England in December
October 1190	Richard captures Messina, Sicily
12 May 1191	Richard marries Berengaria of Navarre
May 1191	Richard captures Cyprus
June 1191	Richard arrives at Acre
20 August 1191	Richard orders the execution of his Muslim prisoners

7 September 1191	Richard defeats the army of Saladin at the battle of Arsuf
August 1192	Richard retakes Jaffa from Saladin
September 1192	Richard and Saladin reach a truce
1192	Returning from crusade, Richard is captured by Duke Leopold of Austria
1194	Richard is released from captivity upon payment of an enormous ransom and returns to England, where he is crowned king for a second time
1194–9	Richard campaigns in France to regain territories lost to King Philip II
1196–8	Richard builds Chateau Gaillard in Normandy
6 April 1199	Richard dies at the siege of Châlus-Chabrol
1204	Eleanor of Aquitaine, Richard's mother, dies
1230	Berengaria of Navarre, Richard's widow, dies

REFERENCES

Introduction: The Life and Times of Richard I

1 Jean Flori, *Richard the Lionheart: King and Knight*, trans. Jean Birrell (Edinburgh, 1999), p. 11.
2 G. N. Garmonsway, trans., *The Anglo-Saxon Chronicle* (London, 1965), p. 265.
3 William of Newburgh, *The History of English Affairs*, ed. and trans. P. G. Walsh and M. J. Kennedy, vol. 1 (Oxford, 1988), p. 128.
4 Richard of Devizes, *The Chronicle of Richard of Devizes of the Time of Richard the First*, ed. John T. Appleby (London, 1963), pp. 25–6.
5 Robert Levine, trans., *A Thirteenth-Century Minstrel's Chronicle (Récits d'un Ménestrel de Reims)* (Lampeter, 1990), pp. 12–13.
6 Flori, *Richard the Lionheart*, p. 42.
7 William D. Paden Jr, Tilde Sankovitch and Patricia H. Stäblein, eds, *The Poems of the Troubadour Bertran de Born* (Berkeley, CA, 1986), p. 218.
8 Gerald of Wales, *Instruction for a Ruler (De principis instructione)*, ed. and trans. Robert Bartlett (Oxford, 2018), p. 479.
9 Roger of Howden, *The Annals of Roger de Hoveden*, trans. Henry T. Riley (London, 1853), vol. II, pp. 63–4.
10 Hilary Rhodes, 'Richard the Lionheart, Contested Queerness, and Crusading Memory', *Open Library of Humanities*, IX/1 (2023), p. 3.
11 The first modern historian to assert that Richard was gay was J. H. Harvey in *The Plantagenets* (London, 1948). Subsequently James Brundage, in *Richard Lion Heart* (New York, 1974), gave the argument full consideration and support. John Gillingham has consistently offered what he considers to be a historicizing corrective to this view (Gillingham, *Richard I*, New Haven, CT, 1999). William Burgwinkle and Hilary Rhodes argue the case for a gay Richard I, while attempting to step out from behind the baggage of the historiographical tradition of writing on the question: William Burgwinkle, *Sodomy, Masculinity and Law in Medieval Literature: France and England, 1050–1230* (Cambridge, 2004), and 'Why It Matters that Richard the Lionheart Was Queer', paper given at the Annual Meeting of the Medieval Academy of

America 2022 (I'm grateful to Professor Burgwinkle for sharing his paper with me); Rhodes, 'Richard the Lionheart, Contested Queerness, and Crusading Memory'. For an interesting discussion of changes in the understanding of heteronormativity in the twelfth century, see Mathew D. Kuefler, 'Male Friendship and the Suspicion of Sodomy in Twelfth-Century France', in *Gender and Difference in the Middle Ages*, ed. Sharon Farmer and Carol Braun Pasternack (Minneapolis, MN, 2003), pp. 145–81.

12 Gerald of Wales, *Instruction for a Ruler*, pp. 611–13.

13 Roger of Howden, *Annals*, p. 110.

14 Matthew Paris, *Chronica majora*, ed. H. R. Luard, vol. II (London, 1874), p. 346.

15 Roger of Howden, *Annals*, p. 118.

16 Ibid., p. 119.

17 These centuries brought the rise of what the historian Robert Moore has termed 'a persecuting society'. R. I. Moore, *The Formation of a Persecuting Society: Power and Deviance in Western Europe, 950–1250* (Oxford, 1987).

18 Paris, *Chronica majora*, II, p. 356.

19 Roger of Howden, *Annals*, pp. 176–7.

20 Flori, *Richard the Lionheart*, p. 134.

21 Marianne Ailes, trans., *The History of the Holy War: Ambroise's 'Estoire de la Guerre Sainte'*, 2 vols (Woodbridge, 2003), vol. II, p. 108.

22 See Gillingham, *Richard I*, p. 232 for a fuller account of the different versions of this story.

23 Geoffrey of Vinsauf, *The New Poetics*, trans. James J. Murphy, in *Three Medieval Rhetorical Arts*, ed. Murphy (Berkeley, CA, 1971), p. 47.

24 Nigel Saul, *The Three Richards: Richard I, Richard II and Richard III* (London, 2005), p. 7.

25 For a description of the historiography on Richard, see Gillingham, *Richard I*, pp. 1–14; Saul, *The Three Richards*, pp. 7–10.

26 Quoted in John Gillingham, *Richard Coeur de Lion: Kingship, Chivalry and War in the Twelfth Century* (London, 1994), p. 95.

27 Helen J. Nicholson, trans., *The Chronicle of the Third Crusade: A Translation of the Itinerarium peregrinorum et gesta regis Ricardi* (Aldershot, 1997), p. 146.

1 Richard I in the Words of His Contemporaries

1 Richard of Devizes, *The Chronicle of Richard of Devizes of the Time of Richard the First*, ed. John T. Appleby (London, 1963), p. 3, quoting Statius, *Thebiad*, i.17. For the avoidance of ambiguity, Richard of Devizes is hereafter referred to as 'Devizes' rather than 'Richard', though the latter is the more conventional manner of referring to him.

2 John of Salisbury, *Historia pontificalis*, trans. Marjorie Chibnall (Oxford, 1986), p. 4.

3 Ibid., p. 3.

4 Antonia Gransden, *Historical Writing in England, c. 500–c. 1307* (London, 1974), p. 219.

5 William of Newburgh, *The History of English Affairs*, ed. and trans. P. G. Walsh and M. J. Kennedy, vol. 1 (Oxford, 1988), p. 27.

6 Hayden White, *Metahistory* (Baltimore, MD, 1973), pp. 7–11.

7 John Gillingham, *Richard Coeur de Lion: Kingship, Chivalry and War in the Twelfth Century* (London, 1994), p. 141.

8 W. L. Warren, *Henry II* (London, 1973), p. 149. See also John Gillingham, *The Angevin Empire* (New York, 1984), and R. I. Moore, *The First European Revolution, c. 970–1215* (Oxford, 2000).

9 He also wrote *De viis maris* (On Sea Voyages), which recounts the stages of his journeys, and perhaps also two similarly travel-orientated texts: *Expositio mappe mundi* (The Explanation of the Map of the World) and *Liber nautarum* (The Book of Sailors).

10 Quoted in Michael Staunton, *The Historians of Angevin England* (Oxford, 2017), p. 114.

11 Henry Bainton, *History and the Written Word: Documents, Literacy, and Language in the Age of the Angevins* (Philadelphia, PA, 2020), p. 19.

12 Ibid., p. 13.

13 Roger of Howden, *The Annals of Roger de Hoveden*, trans. Henry T. Riley (London, 1853), vol. II, pp. 429–30.

14 Ibid., p. 64.

15 Ibid., p. 191.

16 Ibid., p. 192.

17 Ibid., p. 448.

18 Ibid.

19 Ibid., p. 176.

20 Ibid., pp. 176–7.

21 Ibid., p. 356.

22 Ibid., p. 357.
23 Ibid., p. 453.
24 Ibid., p. 454.
25 Appleby, Introduction to Richard of Devizes, *Chronicle*, p. xi.
26 See Marisa Libbon, 'The Function of Twelfth-Century Form in the
   Chronicle of Richard of Devizes', *Viator*, LII/1 (2021), pp. 171–210.
27 Richard of Devizes, *Chronicle*, p. 1.
28 Ibid., p. 2.
29 Richard of Devizes, *Chronicle*, p. xiv.
30 Richard Howlett, ed., *Chronicles of the Reigns of Stephen, Henry II,
   and Richard I* (London, 1884–9), p. cxxii.
31 Richard of Devizes, *Chronicle*, p. 9.
32 Ibid., p. 9.
33 Ibid., p. 4.
34 Ibid., p. 64.
35 Ibid., pp. 68–9.
36 Ibid., p. 65.
37 Ibid., p. 67.
38 Ibid.
39 Ibid., pp. 38–9.
40 Ibid., p. 5.
41 Ibid., p. 39.
42 Ibid., p. 16.
43 Ibid., p. 42.
44 Ibid., p. 43.
45 Ibid., p. 78.
46 Ibid., p. 75.
47 Ibid., pp. 73–4.
48 Ibid., p. 76.
49 Ibid., p. 78.
50 Ibid., p. 77.
51 Ibid., p. 84.
52 Ailes notes that 'his language is Norman, with some overlay from
   an Anglo-Norman scribe' (Marianne Ailes, trans., *The History
   of the Holy War: Ambroise's 'Estoire de la Guerre Sainte'*, 2 vols
   (Woodbridge, 2003), vol. II, p. 2).
53 Ibid., p. 46.
54 Helen J. Nicholson, trans., *The Chronicle of the Third Crusade:
   A Translation of the Itinerarium peregrinorum et gesta regis Ricardi*
   (Aldershot, 1997), and R. C. Johnston, ed., *The Crusade and Death
   of Richard I* (Oxford, 1961).

55 This is, significantly, the form of vernacular romance and hagiography, but not usually of *chanson de geste*, which is written in assonanced *laisses*, or stanzas.

56 Ailes, trans., *History of the Holy War*, p. 50.

57 Ibid., p. 96.

58 Ibid., p. 50.

59 Ibid., p. 37.

60 Paul Bancourt, 'De l'imagerie au réel: L'exoticisme oriental d'Ambroise', *Images et signes de l'Orient dans l'Occident médiéval*, *Senefiance*, xi (1982), pp. 27–39.

61 Ailes, trans., *History of the Holy War*, p. 102.

62 Ibid., p. 30.

63 Ibid., p. 31. My discussion of the representation of Richard as a hero of *chanson de geste* is indebted to Ailes, trans., *History of the Holy War*, and Marianne Ailes, 'Ambroise's *Estoire de la Guerre Sainte* and the Development of a Genre', *Reading Medieval Studies*, xxxiv (2008), pp. 1–19.

64 Ailes, trans., *History of the Holy War*, p. 111.

65 Ibid., pp. 89–90.

66 Ibid., p. 65.

67 Gerald of Wales, *Instructions for a Ruler (De principis instructione)*, ed. and trans. Robert Bartlett (Oxford, 2018), pp. 600–601.

68 Ibid., p. 729.

69 Staunton, *Historians of Angevin England*, p. 2.

2 The Lionheart and the Troubadours

1 Charmaine Lee, 'Richard the Lionheart: The Background to *Ja nus homs pris*', in *Literature of the Crusades*, ed. Simon Thomas Parsons and Linda Paterson (Woodbridge, 2018), pp. 134–49 (p. 136).

2 This account is indebted to Thomas Asbridge, *Richard i: The Crusader King* (London, 2018), pp. 74–5.

3 See John Gillingham, *Richard i* (New Haven, ct, 1999), p. 232 for differing accounts of what gave Richard away.

4 Robert Levine, trans., *A Thirteenth-Century Minstrel's Chronicle (Récits d'un Ménstrel de Reims)*, vol. iv (Lampeter, 1990), p. 28.

5 Ibid.

6 Although some scholars have identified Blondel with a certain Blondel de Nesle, a poet active in the second half of the twelfth century, his role in Richard's rescue is certainly fictive (Yvan Lepage,

'Blondel de Nesle et Richard Coeur de Lion: Histoire d'une legende', *Florilegium*, vii/1 (1985), pp. 109–28).

7 The language is also commonly referred to as 'Provençale', although this term can be misleading, because the territory in which the language was used was much larger than present-day Provence. 'Occitan' comes from the word for 'yes' in this region, *oc*, from which the language was referred to as *langue d'oc*, the language of *oc*.

8 'The *sirventes* was a catch-all genre, a grab-bag of opinions, polemics, insults, the transcription of personal experiences, moral commentary, advice to rulers, praise of kings, and exhortation to the crusades'; Karen Wilk Klein, *The Partisan Voice: A Study of the Political Lyric in France and Germany, 1180–1230* (Paris, 1971), p. 34.

9 Orderic Vitalis, *The Ecclesiastical History*, ed. and trans. Marjorie Chibnall, 6 vols (Oxford, 1975), vol. v, p. 342. See also Gerald A. Bond, ed. and trans., *The Poetry of William vii, Count of Poitiers, ix Duke of Aquitaine* (New York, 1982), p. 240.

10 Bond, *The Poetry*, pp. 29, 11.

11 Ibid., p. 15 (author's translation).

12 William E. Burgwinkle, trans., *Razos and Troubadour Songs* (New York, 1990), pp. 38–9.

13 Anthony Bonner, ed. and trans., *Songs of the Troubadours* (New York, 1972), p. 171.

14 William D. Paden Jr, Tilde Sankovitch and Patricia H. Stäblein, eds, *The Poems of the Troubadour Bertran de Born* (Berkeley, ca, 1986), p. 460.

15 Ibid., p. 338.

16 Margarita Egan, trans., *The Vidas of the Troubadours* (New York, 1984), pp. 17–18.

17 Paden, Sankovitch and Stäblein, eds, *The Poems*, p. 164.

18 Ibid.; Gillingham, *Richard i*, p. 70.

19 Gillingham, *Richard i*, p. 65.

20 Paden, Sankovitch and Stäblein, eds, *The Poems*, p. 182.

21 Ibid., p. 180.

22 Ibid., p. 186.

23 Allen Mandelbaum, trans., *The Divine Comedy of Dante Alighieri: Inferno* (New York, 1982), p. 263.

24 Paden, Sankovitch and Stäblein, eds, *The Poems*, p. 218.

25 Ibid., p. 234.

26 Egan, trans., *The Vidas*, p. 19.

27 Paden, Sankovitch and Stäblein, eds, *The Poems*, p. 236.

28 Ibid., p. 118.

29 Ibid., p. 286.

30 Ibid., p. 430.

31 Ibid., p. 276.

32 Marianne Ailes, trans., *The History of the Holy War: Ambroise's 'Estoire de la Guerre Sainte'*, 2 vols (Woodbridge, 2003), vol. II, p. 174.

33 Stephan Jolie, '"Dauphin, ich möchte Euch zur Rede stellen": Der Lieder des Richard Löwenherz', in *Richard Löwenherz: König – Ritter – Gefangener*, ed. Alexander Schubert (Regensburg, 2017), p. 122.

34 Translation Charmaine Lee 2015, available at https://warwick.ac.uk, accessed 13 October 2024. My discussion of this poem is influenced by that of Lee 'Richard the Lionheart', and of Jolie, 'Der Lieder des Richard'.

35 Lee, 'Richard the Lionheart', p. 138; see also Zingesser's more recent discussion of the relationship between French and Occitan in troubadour manuscripts and scholarship: Eliza Zingesser, *Stolen Song: How the Troubadours Became French* (Ithaca, NY, 2020).

36 Burgwinkle, trans., *Razos and Troubadour Songs*, p. 201.

37 Ibid., p. 203.

38 Klein, *The Partisan Voice*, p. 31.

39 Jean Flori, *Richard the Lionheart: King and Knight*, trans. Jean Birrell (Edinburgh, 1999), p. 239.

40 Ibid.

41 Marisa Libbon, *Talk and Textual Production in Medieval England* (Columbus, OH, 2021), p. 134.

42 Simon Gaunt and Sarah Kay, 'Introduction', in *The Troubadours: An Introduction* (Cambridge, 1999), p. 1.

3 Romancing Richard the Lionheart

1 '*Richard Coeur de Lion*' is a modern title; the romance has various titles in its medieval manuscripts and was first printed as *Kynge Rycharde cuer du lyon* in 1509.

2 For a comprehensive overview of medieval romance and its influence on later literature, see Helen Cooper, *The English Romance in Time* (Oxford, 2004).

3 If an Anglo-Norman romance about Richard the Lionheart existed, it has not survived. One proximate French-language source may be Ambroise's chronicle of Richard's crusade, *Estoire de la Guerre Sainte*

(History of the Holy War); see Marianne Ailes, trans.,
The History of the Holy War: Ambroise's 'Estoire de la Guerre Sainte',
2 vols (Woodbridge, 2003).

4 The text cited throughout is Katherine H. Terrell, ed. and trans.,
Richard Coeur de Lion (Peterborough, ON, 2018).

5 Raluca L. Radulescu and Cory James Rushton, 'Introduction', in
A Companion to Medieval Popular Romance (Woodbridge, 2009),
pp. 1–8 (p. 1).

6 The term 'Saracen' is contentious. It is the word used throughout
medieval literature to describe followers of Islam, or sometimes
'pagans', but medieval literature tends to display little genuine
understanding of the tenets of Islam. Thus scholars are increasingly
tending to understand this term as a pejorative one that should be
used with care. For more on this point, see John V. Tolan, *Saracens:
Islam in the Medieval European Imagination* (New York, 2002), and
especially Shokoofeh Rajabzadeh, 'The Depoliticized Saracen and
Muslim Erasure', *Literature Compass*, XVI/9–10 (2019), e12548.

7 For a longer discussion of these representations, see Jacqueline de
Weever, *Sheba's Daughters: Whitening and Demonizing the Saracen
Woman in Medieval French Epic* (New York, 1998), p. 57; and
Heather Blurton, *Cannibalism in High Medieval English Literature*
(New York, 2007), p. 110.

8 Philida M.T.A. Schellekens, 'An Edition of the Middle English
Romance: *Richard Coeur de Lion*', PhD diss., Durham University,
1989, vol. II, p. 59.

9 These titles are from the Auchinleck, London Thornton, and
Gonville and Caius College manuscripts, respectively.

10 The manuscripts of *Richard Coeur de Lion* have, since the pioneering
work of its early twentieth-century editor, the Austrian scholar
Karl Brunner, been divided into two groups: the *b* group, which
is earlier and more 'historical', and the *a* group, which is later
and has romance elements that seem to have been added to the
original historical core by way of embellishment. This description,
however, is now agreed to be overly schematic and not particularly
descriptive of the manuscript evidence.

11 For the episodic nature of romance, see Elizabeth Allen, 'Episodes',
in *Middle English*, ed. Paul Strohm (Oxford, 2007), pp. 191–206;
and Peter Haidu, 'The Episode as Semiotic Module in Twelfth-
Century Romance', *Poetics Today*, IV/4 (1983), pp. 655–81.

12 Marisa Libbon, *Talk and Textual Production in Medieval England*
(Columbus, OH, 2021), p. 180.

13 Such lists appear in other medieval texts, both romances and also
   devotional works, where they are used to contrast useful religious
   reading to frivolous romance. 'I warn how first at the beginning,/
   I will make no vain speaking/ of deeds of arms nor of love/ As
   minstrels and other jesters do,' warns the author of the *Speculum
   vitae* (Yin Liu, 'Middle English Romance as Prototype Genre',
   Chaucer Review, XL/4 (2006), pp. 335–53 (p. 349)).

14 An exception to this rule are the romances about Godfrey of
   Bouillon, a famous crusader and first king of the Latin kingdom of
   Jerusalem.

15 'Corbaran' and 'Corbaryng' seem to be fictionalizations of Kerbogha,
   an atabeg of Mosul who aided in the defence of Antioch during the
   First Crusade.

16 The timeline suggested here is implausible. Antioch fell during the
   First Crusade in 1098, and Henry II was born in 1133.

17 Other romance heroes have supernatural ancestry, such as Merlin,
   Alexander the Great and the less well-known Sir Gowther.

18 Terrell, *Richard Coeur de Lion*, p. 257.

19 John Gillingham, *Richard I* (New Haven, CT, 1999), p. 252.

20 The College of Arms MS version has R strangle the lion with scarves
   and stab it with a knife provided by Margery; see Peter Larkin, ed.,
   Richard Coeur de Lion (Kalamazoo, MI, 2015), pp. 3 and 244–6.

21 Some manuscripts include, after Richard's subsequent adventure in
   Messina, lines that describe his real bride, Berengaria of Navarre,
   being brought to Sicily by his mother, Eleanor of Aquitaine, for
   their marriage, and subsequently also on crusade, to Acre. See
   Terrell, *Richard Coeur de Lion*, p. 84 nn.1 and 2. See also Larkin, ed.,
   Richard Coeur de Lion, note to l.2040.

22 In fact, it was 'in response to conflicts between his men and local
   citizens [that] Richard sacked Messina'; see Terrell, *Richard Coeur de
   Lion*, p. 78 n.1.

23 Suzanne M. Yeager, *Jerusalem in Medieval Narrative* (Cambridge,
   2009), pp. 74–5.

24 In real life, Philip left the crusade after the siege of Acre.

25 This observation is made by Terrell in *Richard Coeur de Lion*, p. 17.

26 Geraldine Heng, *Empire of Magic: Medieval Romance and the Politics
   of Cultural Fantasy* (New York, 2003), p. 77.

27 Raymond d'Aguilers, *Historia francorum qui ceperunt Iherusalem*, trans.
   John Hugh Hill and Laurita Hill (Philadelphia, PA, 1968), p. 101.

28 There is some anachronism here; Longespée participated in the
   Fourth Crusade.

29 Terrell, *Richard Coeur de Lion*, p. 170 n.1 – and see her appendices.

30 Ailes, trans., *The History of the Holy War*, p. 184.

31 See the exhibition 'Bringing the Holy Land Home: The Crusades, Chertsey Abbey, and the Reconstruction of a Medieval Masterpiece', https://chertseytiles.holycross.edu, accessed 12 March 2025, for a more authentic reproduction of the fragmentary tiles.

32 Roger Sherman Loomis, '*Richard Coeur de Lion* and the *Pas Saladin* in Medieval Art', PMLA, XXX/3 (1915), pp. 509–28.

33 Helen Cooper, 'When Romance Comes True', in *Boundaries in Medieval Romance*, ed. Neil Cartlidge (Woodbridge, 2008), pp. 13–28 (p. 29).

4 The Lionheart and the Prince of Thieves

1 Walter Scott, *The Talisman*, ed. J. B. Ellis (Edinburgh, 2009), p. 3.

2 The preceding account follows Arthur Johnston, *Enchanted Ground: The Study of Medieval Romance in the Eighteenth Century* (London, 1964) and Marisa Libbon, *Talk and Textual Production in Medieval England* (Columbus, OH, 2021).

3 Joseph Ritson, *Robin Hood: A Collection of All the Ancient Poems Songs and Ballads Now Extant, Relative to that Celebrated Outlaw* (London, 1885), p. ii.

4 Roger of Howden, *The Annals of Roger de Hoveden*, trans. Henry T. Riley (London, 1853), vol. II, p. 316.

5 'Robin Hood and the Monk' and 'Robin Hood and the Potter', in *Robin Hood and Other Outlaw Tales*, ed. Stephen Knight and Thomas H. Ohlgren (Kalamazoo, MI, 1997).

6 *The Gest of Robyn Hode*, ibid., ll.1541–2.

7 Ibid., l.1412.

8 Quoted in Stephen Knight and Thomas Ohlgren, eds, *Robin Hood and Other Outlaw Tales*, 2nd edn (Kalamazoo, MI, 2000), p. 27.

9 Author's translation. Ritson (*Robin Hood*, p. ix) cites these lines of Major, thus popularizing this point of view.

10 Jeffrey L. Singman, 'Munday's Unruly Earl', in *Playing Robin Hood: The Legend as Performance in Five Centuries*, ed. Lois Potter (Newark, DE, 1998), pp. 63–76 (pp. 63–4).

11 The discussion above draws mainly on ibid., pp. 63–4, and Knight, 'Robin Hood and the Crusades'.

12 Walter Scott, *Ivanhoe* (Edinburgh, 1998), pp. 65–6.

13 Ibid., p. 124.

14 Ibid., p. 360.

15 Knight, 'Robin Hood and the Crusades', p. 212.

16 Scott, *Ivanhoe*, p. 114.

17 Ibid., p. 143.

18 Ibid., pp. 171 and 169.

19 Ibid., pp. 245 and 261.

20 Ibid., p. 365.

21 Ibid., p. 396.

22 Scott, *The Talisman*, p. 73.

23 Ibid., p. 55.

24 Ibid., p. 56.

25 John Gillingham, *Richard I* (New Haven, CT, 1999), p. 1.
   The discussion that follows depends on ibid., ch. 1: 'The Best
   of Kings, the Worst of Kings'.

26 Quoted ibid., p. 10.

27 Thomas Asbridge, *Richard I: The Crusader King* (London, 2018),
   p. 104.

28 Scott, *Ivanhoe*, p. 192.

29 Robert Henry, *The History of Great Britain, from the Invasions of It
   by the Romans under Julius Caesar*, 6th edn (London, 1823), vol. v,
   p. 228.

30 Katharine M. Morsberger and Robert E. Morsberger, 'Robin Hood
   on Film: Can We Ever Again "Make Them Like They Used To"?',
   in *Playing Robin Hood*, ed. Potter, p. 208.

31 The 1980s television series *Robin of Sherwood* had earlier featured
   an Arab companion for Robin (Stephen Knight, *Robin Hood:
   A Complete Study of the English Outlaw* (Oxford, 1994), p. 243),
   although that character was played by a white English actor.
   This tradition is continued in television adaptations.

32 Edward Said, *Orientalism* (New York, 2003), p. 301.

33 Matthew Richard Schlimm, 'The Necessity of Permanent Criticism:
   A Postcolonial Critique of Ridley Scott's *Kingdom of Heaven*',
   Journal of Media and Religion, IX/3 (2010), pp. 129–49 (p. 131).

34 The costuming throughout the film is a blend of the medieval and
   modern; Robin's hood, for example, is a version of a quilted black
   hoodie sweatshirt.

35 Matt Zoller Seitz, 'Robin Hood' (review), www.rogerebert.com,
   21 November 2018. Another reviewer, David Ehrlich, describes it
   as 'an incoherent deleted scene from *American Sniper* . . . the Iraq
   War parallels so obvious that you half expect Robin to complain
   that he was sent into battle without an exit strategy': '*Robin Hood*

Review: Revisionist History Has Never Been Dumber or More
Boring', www.indiewire.com, 20 November 2018.

Epilogue

1 Jean Flori, *Richard the Lionheart: King and Knight*, trans. Jean Birrell
(Edinburgh, 1999), p. 239.
2 Katherine H. Terrell, ed. and trans., *Richard Coeur de Lion*
(Peterborough, ON, 2018), l.28.
3 Ibid., l.3549.
4 John Gillingham, *Richard the Lionheart* (New York, 1979), pp. 8–9.
5 Thomas Asbridge, *Richard I: The Crusader King* (London, 2018),
p. 104.
6 George Henry Needler, 'Richard Coeur de Lion in Literature',
PhD diss., University of Leipzig, 1890, p. 1.
7 Walter Scott, *Ivanhoe* (Edinburgh, 1998), p. 365.
8 Walter Scott, 'Essay on Chivalry', in *Essays on Chivalry, Romance,
and the Drama* (London, 1887), p. 5.
9 Mark Girouard, *The Return to Camelot: Chivalry and the English
Gentleman* (New Haven, CT, 1981), p. 260.
10 Elizabeth Siberry, *The New Crusaders: Images of the Crusades in the
19th and Early 20th Centuries* (Aldershot, 2000), pp. 150–56.
11 Robert Baden-Powell, *Scouting for Boys* (London, 1908), p. 13.
12 Ibid., p. 243.
13 Roger of Howden, *The Annals of Roger de Hoveden*, trans. Henry
T. Riley (London, 1853), vol. II, p. 454.
14 Nigel Bryant, trans., *The History of William Marshall* (Woodbridge,
2016), p. 150.
15 Philippe Charlier et al., 'The Embalmed Heart of Richard the
Lionheart (1199 AD): A Biological and Anthropological Analysis',
Scientific Reports, III/1296 (2013), pp. 1–6.

SELECT BIBLIOGRAPHY

Primary Sources

d'Aguilers, Raymond, *Historia francorum qui ceperunt Iherusalem*,
  trans. John Hugh Hill and Laurita Hill (Philadelphia, PA, 1968)
Ailes, Marianne, trans., *The History of the Holy War: Ambroise's
  'Estoire de la Guerre Sainte'*, 2 vols (Woodbridge, 2003)
Baden-Powell, Robert, *Scouting for Boys* (London, 1908)
Bond, Gerald A., ed. and trans., *The Poetry of William VII,
  Count of Poitiers, IX Duke of Aquitaine* (New York, 1982)
Bonner, Anthony, ed. and trans., *Songs of the Troubadours*
  (New York, 1972)
Bryant, Nigel, trans., *The History of William Marshall* (Woodbridge,
  2016)
Burgwinkle, William E., trans., *Razos and Troubadour Songs*
  (New York, 1990)
Egan, Margarita, trans., *The Vidas of the Troubadours* (New York, 1984)
Gerald of Wales, *Instruction for a Ruler (De Principis Instructione)*,
  ed. and trans. Robert Bartlett (Oxford, 2018)
John of Salisbury, *Historia pontificalis*, trans. Marjorie Chibnall (Oxford,
  1986)
Johnston, R. C., ed., *The Crusade and Death of Richard I* (Oxford, 1961)
Knight, Stephen, and Thomas H. Ohlgren, eds, *Robin Hood and Other
  Outlaw Tales* (Kalamazoo, MI, 1997)
Larkin, Peter, ed., *Richard Coeur de Lion* (Kalamazoo, MI, 2015)
Levine, Robert, trans., *A Thirteenth-Century Minstrel's Chronicle (Récits
  d'un Ménstrel de Reims)*, Studies in French Civilization, vol. IV
  (Lampeter, 1990)
Nicholson, Helen J., trans., *Chronicle of the Third Crusade: A Translation
  of the Itinerarium peregrinorum et gesta regis Ricardi* (Aldershot, 1997)
Orderic Vitalis, *The Ecclesiastical History*, ed. and trans. Marjorie
  Chibnall, 6 vols (Oxford, 1969–80)
Paden, William D. Jr, Tilde Sankovitch and Patricia H. Stäblein, eds,
  The Poems of the Troubadour Bertran de Born (Berkeley, CA, 1986)
Paris, Matthew, *Chronica majora*, ed. H. R. Luard, 7 vols (London,
  1872–84)

Richard of Devizes, *The Chronicle of Richard of Devizes of the Time of Richard the First*, ed. John T. Appleby (London, 1963)

Ritson, Joseph, *Robin Hood: A Collection of All the Ancient Poems Songs and Ballads Now Extant, Relative to that Celebrated Outlaw* (London, 1885)

Roger of Howden, *The Annals of Roger de Hoveden*, trans. Henry T. Riley, 2 vols (London, 1853)

Scott, Walter, 'Essay on Chivalry', in *Essays on Chivalry, Romance, and the Drama* (London, 1887)

—, *Ivanhoe* (Edinburgh, 1998)

—, *The Talisman*, ed. J. B. Ellis (Edinburgh, 2009)

Terrell, Katherine H., ed. and trans., *Richard Coeur de Lion* (Peterborough, ON, 2018)

William of Newburgh, *The History of English Affairs*, ed. and trans. P. G. Walsh and M. J. Kennedy, 2 vols (Oxford, 1988–2007)

Secondary Sources

Ailes, Marianne, 'Ambroise's *Estoire de la Guerre Sainte* and the Development of a Genre', *Reading Medieval Studies*, XXXIV (2008), pp. 1–19

Asbridge, Thomas, *Richard I: The Crusader King* (London, 2018)

Bainton, Henry, *History and the Written Word: Documents, Literacy, and Language in the Age of the Angevins* (Philadelphia, PA, 2020)

Blurton, Heather, *Cannibalism in High Medieval English Literature* (New York, 2007)

Boyle, David, *The Troubadour's Song: The Capture and Ransom of Richard the Lionheart* (New York, 2005)

Broughton, Bradford, *The Legends of Richard the Lionheart* (The Hague, 1966)

Brundage, James, *Richard Lion Heart* (New York, 1974)

Burgwinkle, William, *Sodomy, Masculinity and Law in Medieval Literature: France and England, 1050–1230* (Cambridge, 2004)

Charlier, Philippe, et al., 'The Embalmed Heart of Richard the Lionheart (1199 AD): A Biological and Anthropological Analysis', *Scientific Reports*, III/1296 (2013), pp. 1–6

Cooper, Helen, *The English Romance in Time* (Oxford, 2004)

Crook, David, *Robin Hood: Legend and Reality* (Woodbridge, 2020)

De Weever, Jacqueline, *Sheba's Daughters: Whitening and Demonizing the Saracen Woman in Medieval French Epic* (New York, 1998)

Flori, Jean, *Richard the Lionheart: King and Knight*, trans. Jean Birrell
    (Edinburgh, 1999)

Gaunt, Simon, and Sarah Kay, eds, *The Troubadours: An Introduction*
    (Cambridge, 1999)

Gillingham, John, *The Angevin Empire* (New York, 1984)

—, *Richard I* (New Haven, CT, 1999)

—, *Richard Coeur de Lion: Kingship, Chivalry and War in the Twelfth
    Century* (London, 1994)

Girouard, Mark, *The Return to Camelot: Chivalry and the English
    Gentleman* (New Haven, CT, 1981)

Gransden, Antonia, *Historical Writing in England, c. 500–c. 1307*
    (London, 1974)

Harvey, J. H., *The Plantagenets* (London, 1948)

Heng, Geraldine, *Empire of Magic: Medieval Romance and the Politics of
    Cultural Fantasy* (New York, 2003)

Johnston, Arthur, *Enchanted Ground: The Study of Medieval Romance
    in the Eighteenth Century* (London, 1964)

Klein, Karen Wilk, *The Partisan Voice: A Study of the Political Lyric
    in France and Germany, 1180–1230* (Paris, 1971)

Knight, Stephen, *Robin Hood: A Complete Study of the English Outlaw*
    (Oxford, 1994)

—, 'Robin Hood and the Crusades: When and Why Did the
    Longbowman of the People Mount Up Like a Lord?', *Florilegium*,
    XXIII/1 (2006), pp. 201–22

Kuefler, Mathew D., 'Male Friendship and the Suspicion of Sodomy
    in Twelfth-Century France', in *Gender and Difference in the Middle
    Ages*, ed. Sharon Farmer and Carol Braun Pasternack (Minneapolis,
    MN, 2003), pp. 145–81

Lee, Charmaine, 'Richard the Lionheart: The Background to
    Ja nus homs pris', in *Literature of the Crusades*, ed. Simon Thomas
    Parsons and Linda Paterson (Woodbridge, 2018), pp. 134–49

Libbon, Marisa, 'The Function of Twelfth-Century Form in
    the Chronicle of Richard of Devizes', *Viator*, LII/1 (2021),
    pp. 171–210

Liu, Yin, 'Middle English Romance as Prototype Genre', *Chaucer
    Review*, XL/4 (2006), pp. 335–53

Mitchell, Jerome, *Scott, Chaucer and Medieval Romance: A Study in
    Sir Walter Scott's Indebtedness to the Literature of the Middle Ages*
    (Lexington, KY, 1987)

Moore, R. I., *The Formation of a Persecuting Society: Power and Deviance
    in Western Europe, 950–1250* (Oxford, 1987)

Needler, George Henry, 'Richard Coeur de Lion in Literature',
    PhD diss., University of Leipzig, 1890

Nelson, Janet L., ed., *Richard Coeur de Lion in History and Myth*
    (London, 1992)

Potter, Lois, ed., *Playing Robin Hood: The Legend as Performance
    in Five Centuries* (Newark, NJ, 1998)

Radulescu, Raluca L., and Cory James Rushton, *A Companion to
    Medieval Popular Romance* (Woodbridge, 2009)

Rajabzadeh, Shokoofeh, 'The Depoliticized Saracen and Muslim
    Erasure', *Literature Compass*, XVI/9–10 (2019), e12548

Rhodes, Hilary, 'Richard the Lionheart, Contested Queerness, and
    Crusading Memory', *Open Library of Humanities*, IX/1 (2023),
    pp. 1–20

Richard Coeur de Lion: Entre Mythe et réalités (Ghent, 2016)

Saul, Nigel, *The Three Richards: Richard I, Richard II and Richard III*
    (London, 2005)

Schlimm, Matthew Richard, 'The Necessity of Permanent Criticism:
    A Postcolonial Critique of Ridley Scott's *Kingdom of Heaven*',
    Journal of Media and Religion, IX/3 (2010), pp. 129–49

Schubert, Alexander, ed., *Richard Löwenherz: König – Ritter – Gefangener*
    (Regensburg, 2017)

Siberry, Elizabeth, *The New Crusaders: Images of the Crusades in the
    19th and Early 20th Centuries* (Aldershot, 2000)

Simmons, Clare A., *Reversing the Conquest: History and Myth in
    Nineteenth-Century British Literature* (New Brunswick, NJ, 1990)

Staunton, Michael, *The Historians of Angevin England* (Oxford, 2017)

Tolan, John V., *Saracens: Islam in the Medieval European Imagination*
    (New York, 2002)

Turner, Ralph V., and Richard R. Heiser, *The Reign of Richard Lionheart:
    Ruler of the Angevin Empire, 1189–1199* (Harlow, 2000)

Zingesser, Eliza, *Stolen Song: How the Troubadours Became French*
    (Ithaca, NY, 2020)

ACKNOWLEDGEMENTS

My warmest thanks are due to Christine Chism, who recommended me for this project: her intellectual generosity and collegiality are a much valued feature of the southern California medieval community. I'd like also to thank the participants in the California Medieval History Seminar at the University of California, Los Angeles, for their generous comments on a draft of the Introduction. University of California, Santa Barbara undergraduate students in the Faculty Research Assistance Program provided welcome guidance on the representation of *Richard the Lionheart* and Robin Hood in video games and other new media. Brian Donnelly, as ever, is my first and best reader. Finally, I gratefully acknowledge the editors at Reaktion Books for their support: Michael Leaman, Alex Ciobanu and Amy Salter. All errors remain my own. This *Richard the Lionheart: In Life and in Legend* is dedicated to my dad, in the hope that he might read this one!

PHOTO ACKNOWLEDGEMENTS

The author and publishers wish to express their thanks to the sources listed below for illustrative material and/or permission to reproduce it. Some locations of artworks are also given below, in the interest of brevity:

AdobeStock: pp. 6 (dbrnjhrj), 14 (rysan34), 39 (alisonallenphoto), 68 (Tina Binder), 103 (Rostislav Ageev), 129 (Oliver Hlavaty), 132 (Markus S.), 166 (wjarek); Biblioteca Apostolica Vaticana, Vatican City (Vat. Lat. 5232, fol. 203r): p. 84; Bibliothèque nationale de France, Paris: pp. 25 (MS Français 2813, fol. 238v), 75 (MS Français 12473, fol. 128r); British Library, London: pp. 43 (Royal MS 16 G VI, fol. 347v), 69 (Cotton MS Vitellius A XIII, fol. 5r), 127 (Add MS 42130, fol. 82r); The British Museum, London: p. 126; Burgerbibliothek, Bern (Cod. 389, fol. 83v): p. 74; collection of the author: p. 160; Corpus Christi College, Cambridge: pp. 17 (MS 26, fol. 140r), 49 (MS 339, fol. 38r); from *The Eglinton Tournament* (London, 1843), photo Harold B. Lee Library, Brigham Young University, Provo, UT: p. 163; from John Richard Green, *A Short History of the English People* (London, 1876), photo Library of Congress, Washington, DC: p. 10; Heritage Auctions, HA.com: p. 152; Houghton Library, Harvard University, Cambridge, MA: p. 136; Kunstgewerbemuseum, Staatliche Museen zu Berlin/Karen Bartsch (CC BY-SA 4.0): p. 29; Médiathèque du patrimoine et de la photographie, Charenton-le-Pont, photo RMN-Grand Palais/Henri Heuzé/RMN-GP/Dist. SCALA, Florence: p. 165; The Morgan Library & Museum, New York: pp. 100 (PML 20931), 119 (MS M.638, fol. 23v); Museum für Islamische Kunst, Staatliche Museen zu Berlin/Johannes Kramer (CC BY-SA 4.0): p. 60; National Library of Scotland, Edinburgh (Adv. MS 19.2.1, fol. 326r): p. 118; from *Pictures of English History* (London, 1868), photo George A. Smathers Libraries, University of Florida, Gainesville: p. 66; Real Biblioteca del Monasterio de San Lorenzo de El Escorial, courtesy Patrimonio Nacional: pp. 46 (MS Vitrinas 1, fol. 23r), 72 (MS B-I-2, fol. 162r); Shutterstock.com: p. 47 (Sissoupitch); The University of Edinburgh (CC BY 3.0): p. 133.

INDEX